running a business doesn't come with a manual...but it does now!

The A-Z for Business Development and Success.

niki matyjasik

Copyright © 2022 by Niki Matyjasik

ISBN13 Paperback: 979-8-356243-60-8

ISBN13 Hardback: 978-1-915771-04-9

All rights reserved.

No part of this book may be reproduced in any form or by any electronic or mechanical means, including information storage and retrieval systems, without written permission from the author, except for the use of brief quotations in a book review.

contents

FOREWORD	7
INTRODUCTION	9
PART A: MAKING A PLAN	19
Reflect on Where You Are	19
Passions and Procrastinations	21
Procrastinations	24
Plan, Do, Review, and Improve	25
Vision	33
Why is Goal Setting Important?	36
PART B: MOVING FORWARD WITH PURPOSE	40
Your Story	40
What is Your Why and purpose for Running Your Business?	41
The Accountability Toolkit	42
Distractions and Unexpected Situations	48
Follow Your Plan	50
Summary of Suggested Strategies to Avoid Distractions and Deviations	51
Summary: How to Move Forward in Business	52
PART C: MANAGING AREAS OF YOUR BUSINESS	56
Sales and Marketing, People, Operations, Finance	56
Sales and Marketing	57
Visibility Strategy	60
Networking	65
People	76
Operations	77
Finance	90

PART D: A-Z BUSINESS GUIDE	103
PART E: THERE IS NO MAGIC SECRET	163
ACKNOWLEDGEMENTS	167
WORK WITH NIKI	169
ABOUT THE AUTHOR	171

dedication

For my husband Lance and daughter Charlotte for always being there for me, supporting me every step of the way on my business and personal journey.

For my Matyjasik family, in particular Sarah and Cazzie, for your ongoing love, support, and cheerleading, and for showing me unconditional love and loads of hugs! I don't know where I would be without you all.

For my amazing clients, raving fans, and support network. You have been an absolute delight and an honour to work with. Thank you for always having the faith in me that I can support you, hold the space for you, build a plan and strategy for you and kick you up the bum! (In a nice way – to keep you on track!)

And for every single entrepreneur and business owner! Well done for being in this space. It's tough and challenging to run a business... yet rewarding. I salute you all: it ain't easy, but we've got this!

foreword

Having worked side-by-side with Niki for eighteen months – and counting – the world needs to hear that there's no sugar coating the rubbish times.

What I'd like you to feel when you read these words is the assurance that you're in the right place to avoid the pitfalls of starting up and running an unsuccessful business.

Business is not a single line to success, it is a wibbly wobbly journey to the highest of highs and the lowest of lows.

And Niki doesn't shy away from any of it.

When you're down she is sleeves rolled up, in there with you, planning to get you up and out. She is holding you to account so you stick to your plans.

And when you're on top, she'll be the first to raise a glass of champagne in celebration of you and everything you have achieved.

foreword

She walks her talk and makes good on all the lessons that business has thrown at her. She operates from a place of extreme integrity with a no-nonsense, kind but firm approach that is essential for entrepreneurial success.

Yes, sure you could enlist an expert who panders to your every word.

But would you grow in that environment?

Nope.

Niki is a growth expert.

Having been in Niki's network for five years (and oh, wow, what a network that is!), having had weekly calls with her, heard her speak in multiple venues, situations, and occasions, it's needless to say that I know what her message is all about.

However, I never fail to learn a truly golden nugget of business advice each and every time she speaks.

Niki is fiercely generous with her time and knowledge so get a highlighter and some post-it notes, read the book, get on her mailing list and absorb everything that Niki has to offer.

Sarah Newland

Sustainable Operations Consultant

Keyboard Smash

introduction

Business owners come to me when they feel overwhelmed and frustrated. They are always busy, yet are not making progress in their business, and they know they need help. They realise that they cannot do it on their own any longer. They are either procrastinating, being inconsistent, being a perfectionist or lacking the motivation to take their plans forward. Sometimes imposter syndrome has kicked in and they believe they aren't up to the job.

They recognise that they need a place to offload what is going on in their heads. They need to share it with someone. They want to work through ideas and produce a plan. Most of all they want to follow a process and structure that will help them every step of the way. They want to be supported by someone who understands them, listens to them, challenges them, connects them to their desires and dreams, and is with them every step of the way as they gain clarity, confidence and, most importantly, the results.

introduction

By results, I mean a consistent monthly income and consistent monthly success – whatever that means to you. This is how to create a business that lasts beyond the first two years.

To establish the next steps and a plan in your business, it is important to have a sounding board, a structure, and a process to follow. You need to be listened to in a space where you can process the plans and ideas in your head. When you have this, you can start to take action. What you gain is *clarity*. You begin to see that your ideas are possible – you just need a solid plan and someone to believe in you. I can always see the potential in others way before they realise it themselves.

All this is summed up in the three key principles that a lot of business owners forget:

1. Take consistent action.
2. Have a robust plan with clear goals.
3. Get some accountability.

This book is for you if you know you'd be able to achieve more by intentionally leveraging the power of accountability and consistency.

Over the past seven years I have helped thousands of small business owners. I have supported them to get clear on their plan and get clear on their goals. I hold their hand and give them a metaphorical kick up the bum to help them achieve

introduction

consistent results. I support them to get the business, life, and balance they are looking for. My approach is to challenge them with a focused and direct approach to allow them to reach the right decisions for them and their business. Once they are on that path, they start to build confidence and belief in themselves. Then the results start to show. The momentum and flow kick in. The snowball effect takes place.

In this book I will share with you my four-step process, Plan, Do, Review, and Improve, plus a nice large dose of accountability and consistency. Sounds simple, right? But you would be surprised at the number of business owners who give up too easily.

I hear things like:

- I am not getting the enquiries I want.
- I don't know my business numbers.
- This is just not working!
- How hard can it be?
- This networking idea is not bringing the clients in that I want.
- I am just too busy to work on my business.
- Why is that business 'over there' doing so much better than me?
- How do I raise my profile?
- What prices should I charge?

The list goes on. I have heard it all.

introduction

The key factors here are: be clear on your plan; be clear on your goals with focus, passion, and motivation; be held accountable; finally, consistency is key.

I work in ninety-day cycles with my clients. You really need this length of time to see what is working and what is not working. Working in a cycle of this length lets you see what your stats say and where your clients are coming from.

A lot of business owners float from one month to the next without reviewing the previous month, without improving on any mistakes, learnings, challenges, or costs to their business. This is why the Review and Improve stages of my four-step process are so crucial.

I am living proof that this process works. I firmly believe in walking my talk. I have either done or have experience of everything I share in my business.

When I first started my business seven years ago, I did not have two pennies to rub together. I was significantly in debt, and I had no Plan B, but I wanted to build a business that would fit around my family. With my background in corporate buying and project management, network marketing and working with an education provider, I knew I had tons of experience to share. I was at a crossroads regarding what I wanted to do, when I came across a networking group called *Women Mean Biz*. It was full of likeminded, supportive, friendly business owners who were all sharing the same challenges and pain points in their businesses. And I knew I could help them.

I had an extremely limited budget, but I decided to invest in networking and give it my all. I decided to network like my life depended on it. I got to know businesses and the people in them, and I built relationships with them. I soon became a leader of one of the networking groups, visited other groups within the network and put myself forward for keynote speaking slots. I have never looked back. Networking is still a key part of my marketing today.

My whole business has been built on the foundations of word of mouth, recommendation, and referral. Even my enquiries through social media have a link back to someone we jointly know. I am hugely passionate about helping small business owners achieve their goals and dreams. By working with me they achieve that and get consistent results. My extensive network means they are able to find me in order for that to happen.

Fast forward seven years: through investing in coaching, masterminding, and personal development, along with drawing on my own experience, perspective, knowledge, expertise, and my four-step process, my business has grown from being £50k in debt to consistent five-figure months.

Sounds impressive, eh? However, it came with a lot of hard work, focus, determination, making mistakes, consistent

introduction

activity, planning, being clear on my goals and having a sounding board with a structure for me to follow.

My promise to you is that if you consistently apply into your business what I share with you in this book, you will do more, achieve more, leverage more, and achieve the results you are looking for.

Here are a few of my favourite quotations to help bring this together. They are so true, particularly when applied in business:

> *"The fortune is in the follow up."*

> *"Your comfort zone is a wonderful place, but nothing ever grows there."*

> *"A year from now, you'll wish you'd started today."*

Running a business hasn't ever come with a manual… until now! I hope this book will give you the space, the solutions, the ideas, and the insights to enable you to take the next steps you need to succeed in your business.

This book is designed to enable you to get clarity and understanding. You'll realise that you are not alone in your difficulties: there are others experiencing the same feelings of demotivation, unclear decision making, and overwhelm. This book will move you towards the clear actions, decisions, activities, and plans that you need to put in place to move you towards your goals.

When you start out as a business owner, not everything falls into place straight away. It takes time, it takes energy, it takes focus, it takes motivation, and it takes effort – and it's about showing up on a regular basis even when you don't feel like it. It is not like an employed job where you can ask the finance person, the operations person, or the accountant to just sort a problem out for you. Particularly when you start out, you are everything to everybody in your business. You've got to deal with the enquiries, the marketing, and the social media. You become the copywriter, the accountant, and the networker. The list of roles goes on, not to mention the fact that you are responsible for finding *and* serving your clients too.

Whatever success you want to achieve, this book will help you break it down in an easy, manageable way so you can see exactly how to plan, review, and improve for consistent results.

There will be discussion of process and how to document all the areas of your business with your systems, your process, and your structure, and how to get them working efficiently for you at any stage of your business journey.

There will also be content about outsourcing in your business. This shouldn't be done lightly, but you can work to get it done in the most effective way. This means being clear on

introduction

what you need someone to do, how long it's going to take them and how much it's going to cost you. Time and time again, business owners bring people in to cover certain areas of their business and it's a waste of time, it's a waste of money, and it's a waste of effort and energy as it is not clear how they are benefitting the business. When you approach outsourcing in the right way you can get much more done, more effectively.

This book will take you on a journey to enable you to get the right structure in place for you and your business... but you must show up and be consistent.

Do we have a deal? We are going to look at:

- My four-step process: Plan, Do, Review, and Improve
- Seeing the opportunity in everything
- Building relationships
- Making key connections
- Getting a support network that's got your back
- Going that extra mile
- Becoming consistent
- Understanding your numbers and stats
- Accountability measures to keep you on track
- Having somebody as a sounding board
- Stealing someone else's belief in you until you find your own
- Being positive and using the Law of Attraction
- Showing up and holding your nerve

introduction

- Creating the results, you are looking for
- Finding the right solutions for you and your business
- Imposter syndrome and comparing
- Chasing the shiny objects
- Sticking by what you say you're going to do
- Gaining control of the overwhelm

Let us take that leap of faith together, step forward and allow this book and process to guide you, support you and encourage you.

You are ready to take your business to where you want it to be. Each chapter will give you a clear action plan to work on to help take you forward.

Trust in yourself, believe in yourself, and roll your sleeves up and get to work. More importantly, have some fun with this process!

part a: making a plan

reflect on where you are

Before you start using my four-step plan, take time to answer these questions, either using a journal or a notebook.

Start with simply answering yes or no. Reflect on the answers. This will help guide you to your starting point. From there, you will have the clarity to move on to make plans which will improve your business.

Success can mean a lot of different things to a lot of different people. In answering these questions, the only important definition of success is what it means to you.

* * *

- Do you plan for success?
- Do you follow through on your plans?
- Do the results in your business match your efforts?
- Are you generating the leads/enquiries you want?
- Are you converting the sales you want?
- Are you moving your business forward consistently?
- Are you satisfied with the amount of progress you've made in your business so far this year?
- Are you willing to make changes in your business?
- Are you looking for support in your business?
- Are you looking for help to make clear decisions in your business?
- Are you serious about keeping your business on track and getting it to where you want it to be?
- Do you need tools to support you in your business moving forward?
- Do you let yourself off the hook too often?
- Are you serious about growing your business?
- Would you achieve more and faster if you intentionally leveraged the power of accountability in your business?

Your answers to these questions can make you feel uncomfortable and stretched outside of your comfort zone. This means you are open to learning and getting support with making key decisions and moving your business forward. It also means you are serious about making changes and creating consistent results.

passions and procrastinations

I bring you good news and bad news. Let's start with the bad news and then we can move on.

It takes a lot to run a business. We need to dedicate time and energy to it, and we might feel like we're winging it. We feel uncomfortable when we leave our comfort zone, and we can give up too easily. We come up against challenges and we don't know what the answers are.

We are passionate about the difference we want to make in the world, and we speak out about what we believe in, but others judge us and do not believe in us. We lose clarity and confidence because business turns out not to be as straightforward as we thought. We might feel lonely, overwhelmed, stuck, or blocked, and lose our focus and motivation.

This leads to not showing up and not being consistent with our activities. Alternatively, we might be persistent, but in the wrong way. It might feel a bit 'icky'. We might not show up and get our products and services out there because we want them to be perfect before anyone sees them. We might get imposter syndrome, thinking that we aren't qualified to sell what we can do for people.

We might experience fear of missing out and jump on the nearest passing bandwagon, attracted by shiny objects. Perhaps we make mistakes but don't learn from them, because we tell ourselves we don't have time for planning and reviewing.

We feel like we need to be personally in control of all aspects of our business, yet we don't have a handle on our numbers, we're not setting clear boundaries, and we lack solid foundations to our business.

These difficulties explain why many businesses fail within their first year or the first three years. A lot of these failures are down to a lack of guidance, a lack of support and solutions, a lack of advice, a lack of vision, goals, and a plan, as well as a lack of funding for small business owners to really get off the ground.

So many of us give up on our dreams because it's just so hard.

But I'd also love to share with you all the good things that you can get from running your business.

You get to follow your passion. You can be your own boss. You have the freedom to run a business where, how, and when you want to – over the past few years we've really proven how possible that is!

You can have a clear mission which supports the values that are important to you. The results that you get for your clients can change their lives, and you get to choose which people you help. You can form great relationships and friendships with likeminded business owners and clients.

You can create a business structure that works for you. You

can set your own income, hours, and holidays. There's nobody to tell you what sort of business you have to create, how much you may earn or what time you may take off.

Does that sound more like it? Are you excited now? Are you excited to move forward and start building this business?

To keep moving in your business and to get the best from this book, identify a few key principles:

- What are you good at? This is what you really want to focus on in your business.
- What are you passionate about? Is this currently reflected in your business?
- What do you really want to achieve?
- What kind of success do you want in your business? Does that relate to where you want to be in your life (whether that regards your family, your loved ones or earning a certain income)?

Passions

This is the first of two questions I ask my clients as soon as we start working together:

What are you most passionate about in your business and life?

To find the driving force for your focus, motivation, and momentum, take the time out to reflect and list what is important to you in your business and *why* you do what you do. When times are tough, this can bring you back to what you are truly passionate about.

What are *your* passions in your business and life? Take a few moments to gather your thoughts and answer below:

Passions

Business

1.

2.

3.

Life/Personal

1.

2.

3.

procrastinations

The second question I ask is:

What do you procrastinate over the most in business and life?

The most common answer I get is *Numbers*. Anything related to accounts has to be a clear winner.

Once you identify these answers, it could be a game changer in your business. When you run your business, you are everything to everyone. This means you end up doing tasks and activities that you really don't like. You can end up doing these until you find the time, money, and energy to outsource. And it could be the thing you procrastinate over in your business which is stopping you from progressing and making clearer decisions.

What do you procrastinate over? Answer below:

Procrastinations

Business

1.

2.

3.

Life/Personal

1.

2.

3.

Now take some time to reflect. Ask yourself, "Are these points really stopping me from moving forward in my business?"

plan, do, review, and improve

This part of the manual breaks down the four-step process of Plan, Do, Review, and Improve.

Plan

Planning can invoke different meanings for different people. When it comes to planning in your business, look at it simply as a process to help you take action to achieve your goals. Planning can be very in depth but can also be a couple of bullet points which summarise what you're hoping to achieve.

Planning at the end of your month for the month ahead means being clear on your goals and where you want to be in thirty days' time. Start with that, whether it is a financial, business, personal or learning goal to help you achieve your overall annual goal.

You can then break down the activities you need to do to be able to achieve the goal that you have set.

Here are two questions to ask yourself when you are setting your goals:

1. How much do I *need* to generate every single month?
2. How much do I *want* to generate every single month?

To create a space between these two figures, use a strategy called *good, better, best*.

For example:

You might set a goal to sign up new retainer clients by the end of the month.

Good...   two new clients

Better...   four new clients

Best...   six new clients

To help you achieve this goal, you might use these activities:

1. Connect with my wait list.
2. Speak to my network about my retainer offer and ask if they know anyone it would help.
3. Connect with my warm leads and make personal outreach calls.

As I have mentioned, I work in ninety-day cycles with my clients. I recommend setting aside a day or half day to plan your next ninety days. Start with your goals, then identify the activities you need to do each month to achieve those goals. Depending on how you like to work, you can break this down into weekly or even daily activities to achieve that goal.

Lots more advice about time management will follow but for now, suffice to say that once you have created the plan, you have to do it!

To access the Plan, Do, Review, Improve workbook:

https://links.nikimatyjasik.co.uk/workbook

Do

From your plan you will have a list of broken-down tasks that you need to complete every day, week, or month to reach your goals.

If this is the first time that you are undertaking a structured approach to planning, you may need to make some adjustments in the Do section as you realise you have more or less time than your plan allows for.

If you are more used to planning, you may have more of an idea about how long the tasks will take you.

Don't worry if you get this wrong and you overestimate what you can get done. This is what the Review section is for. More on that shortly.

Of course, as well as doing all the jobs in your business, you also have to work for your clients and spend time getting more clients in. With that in mind, here is a question that lots of clients have about time:

How Do I Address the Capacity in My Business?

In other words, do you have the capacity to deliver the elements of your plan?

Are your financial goals realistic, considering the time that it will take you to deliver client work and to bring through the leads you have in your pipeline?

If not, do you have any plans in place to learn about and introduce passive or semi-passive income streams?

When Do I Work Best?

When are the best times in the day, week, and month for you to work?

Are you affected by the seasons?

Use this knowledge of yourself to identify the best time to plan, the best time to do the activity, and the best time to review your plans and make your next set of plans.

If there is a particular season or time of year that works best for you, make sure that you have planned that in accordingly.

Complete the activity that you need to achieve your business goals. It's essential to work it back to activity that is *income-producing* activity. In other words, how does this activity translate to the number of enquiries and conversions that you need to achieve the goals that you have set?

Being clear on numbers here is important.

You Don't Have to Be Perfect

Perfectionism can freeze us into fear of moving anything forward. We can have a situation in which we create things in our business, but we don't want to get it out there because we're comparing ourselves adversely with others.

You might not want to be seen as the person who puts something less than perfect out there. This comes back to confidence and clarity. I'm giving you permission to have a JFDI attitude! Get it out there because the worst that can happen is that someone doesn't buy it, and that you don't get quite the outcome you were expecting.

But if you get it out there, you can at least learn from it and understand what is and isn't working.

On the other hand, it could be amazing, and it could absolutely get the results that you were looking for. So don't hide behind perfectionism. If you feel that this is an area in your business or self-development that is holding you back, then reach out to a trusted individual to help you work through it. It can be an absolute game changer when you move things forward rather than waiting for the perfect moment.

What Do I Commit to Do This Week?

If you need a very simple way to work on your priorities when time gets on top of you, you can ask yourself this question: "What do I commit to doing this week?"

This question helps you to work out what is non-negotiable. This way, you can start to work towards your goals this week, month and for your ninety-day cycle. To make this work better, you can find an accountability buddy to help you stay on track with those tasks.

Review

At the end of each month, set aside time to review the month's goals. Ask these questions:

- What are the top three successes from my month?
- What are the top three learnings from my month?
- What three things do I want to improve in the month ahead?

It is important to spend time understanding and developing these areas. You can also highlight, during the course of the month, in the moment, what has worked well in the business and what you've learnt so that you can move forward with the right set of plans as your approach improves. By doing this you can make sure that you are on track with where you want to be and what you are looking to implement.

If there have been any challenges, mistakes, or costs to you that just haven't gone well, you can address them at this point and improve on them in the plan in the month ahead.

Track Your Progress.

It is important to be able to track your progress on a very regular basis when it comes to the month end. Then you can complete your monthly review or the ninety-day planning with ease.

A review at the end of the month should take no more than ten to thirty minutes if everything is in place with your plans and activities.

Daily, weekly, monthly, and seasonal dips occur in business. Having this review structure in place allows you to identify those peaks and troughs. You'll have the information to reflect on month-on-month, year-on-year how your business is performing.

Doing this consistently allows you to plan effectively and put the right structure in place.

Improve

In your overview at the end of the month, you will have reviewed the following:

- Your business numbers
- How many clients you have seen
- How many one-to-ones you have held
- How many enquiries you have received
- Your conversion rates
- Your turnover and profit against the targets you set

This is where you must start getting comfortable with your numbers. Remember your target goals? This is where you get to look at exactly how close you have been to reaching them.

When you understand your conversion rate, you can set your goal for the next month regarding how many conversations you need to have. When you spend time identifying what conversations you need to prioritise in your pipeline, this gives you focus and helps you to set a target, so you avoid procrastinating on those conversations.

An accountability buddy comes in handy with these tasks. Pick a business friend or colleague who is happy to check in on you and hold you to account on those tasks you know you're going to struggle to do.

The overview directly feeds your plan for the next month. If you have created a ninety-day plan, this will help you see what activities need to be tweaked to make sure you don't make the same mistakes or underachieve on your growth potential.

vision

When I started my business, I didn't start with a vision. On reflection, I wish I had.

When you start out in business you are so excited to have what you think you need in place: a website, social media, a new notebook, and essential stationery. But if you don't have your vision in place, you can easily start to drift off track with no clear focus on where you want to be.

A vision is setting a vivid mental image of something that is not perceived as real and is not present to the senses.

You can read all the books, meditate, take yourself off to a quiet place to make a business plan. My advice is to block time out that you will spend dreaming and getting words and imagery to your vision – because it's a lot simpler if it is broken down.

A lot of business owners are coming out of the corporate world or getting into business after having children. It can be hard to find the time to create something as *'woo woo'* as a vision.

However, a clear vision in your life and business is important.

Having a clear vision allows you to steer in the right direction. It brings clarity to where you see your life and business taking you.

A vision encompasses where you see your future. It is out in front of you, and you strive to achieve it. It sets the way for creating goals, mindset, beliefs, values, ethos, and a mission statement. You will not create it within minutes or overnight, so block out time to focus on creating this fully.

Creating Vision Boards

When you do this task for the first time, take a poster-sized piece of paper, different coloured post it notes and a selection of coloured pens. Split the sheet into four sections and ask yourself what you would choose in the following areas if you could have anything, be anything, do anything:

part a: making a plan

- Business
- Personal
- Passion project
- If money were no object

From this, start to take those words and form a vision board either with pictures or using a tool such as Canva or Pinterest. Ensure that the board is visible in a few different places to help you stay focused.

- Put it on your wall.
- Put it on your fridge.
- Put it on your wallpaper – phone or laptop.
- Share it with your family.
- Commit to the board with an accountability buddy.

Tips to Complete the Board.

Think about what you want to achieve, and if you start today what small changes you can make towards that. Spend time imagining that your vision has already come true. Focus on how you feel about that. Plan to use affirmations related to your vision and goals (to be found in the A-Z section).

Create a Day in Your Ideal Life

As you did when making your vision board, take a sheet of poster-sized paper. Consider these questions and follow the exercise.

- Where are you?
- Who are you with?
- What does your business look like?
- What does your personal life look like?
- What are your favourite things to do? (hobbies, activities, etc.)

If you and I were talking in a year's time, what would you want to have happened over the previous twelve months for you to be satisfied with your personal and professional development?

Take a leisurely walk through a day that would be perfect if it represented your typical day – not a holiday, not a 'special' day, but the very substance of your life as you would love it to be. Write this in the present tense and in detail, from getting up in the morning to going to sleep at night. Don't put down only the possible – you have absolute freedom, unlimited means, and all the skills and power you've ever wished for.

Complete this task in either a written version or with pictures or with a drawing. Keep it to hand to remind you on a regular basis why you do what you do and to keep you focused.

why is goal setting important?

Goals move you and your business forward.

Having a goal written down or having a visual (such as a vision board) provides the pathway to achieving it. If a goal is not written down, it can remain only a dream and you might not follow it through.

You are more likely to achieve a goal if it is written down or you have a picture. It is also very important to set a date.

When creating a goal, ask yourself, "When I look back on this in thirty days' time, how will I know I've achieved it?" If there is no measure of success in place, you know that needs to be worked on.

It doesn't have to be perfect the first time; give it a try and review and improve at the end of each month.

Setting SMART Goals

SMART stands for Specific, Measurable, Achievable, Relevant, Timely.

When setting goals, you have a much greater chance of achieving them if you follow a structure.

Specific – State exactly what you want to achieve (who, what, where and why).

Measurable – How will you demonstrate and evaluate the extent to which you have met the goal?

Achievable – Is the goal stretching and challenging? Is it within your ability to achieve the outcome?

Relevant – How does the goal relate to your key responsibilities and objectives?

Timely – Set a deadline against your goals to challenge you and keep you on track.

Note: By following this structure, you can be clear on your goals. In order to reach your goal, you can identify activities that will get you there... but make sure the activities aren't part of the goal itself.

An example goal could be: Achieve an additional £1000 income into the business by the end of the month.

Example activities that will get you there:

- Break down the £1000 across your services and offers.
- Identify how many clients you need for each service.
- Post the offers/services on social media, saying how many spaces are available.
- Set up a measure to stay on track with the numbers.

Each month, carry out your goal planning to align to your vision.

Goals

In summary, when you are setting goals choose one business goal, one personal goal, and one financial goal. Make sure your goals match the SMART criteria. Consider whether you can apply the method of *good, better, best*.

part a: making a plan

Finally, check that the activity is not part of the goal. Activities help you reach your goal: they are not the goal in themselves.

From Plan, Do, Review, and Improve through to Vision and Goals, all these steps are interlinked and flow very well when aligned.

When you complete these steps on a consistent basis, you have the foundation of a business that is efficient and flowing.

part b: moving forward with purpose

your story

When building a business and reaching clients, remember that people buy people. They connect with your personality and what you have said, which allows them to decide whether you are a good fit and if they want to work with you.

Building and practising your story for your business will allow you to share with everybody who you are, what you do and why you do it.

You can use your story in the various ways. You could use it to engage with business owners before a networking event. It could form part of your conversation with your prospects or new clients. You could use it when you give presentations to others.

Use this list of questions as prompts to help you find the basis of your story to share with others:

- What is your name?
- What is your background?
- What do you do and for whom?
- What is your passion?
- What is your vision?
- What attracted you to launching/building your business?
- Why is it so important to you?
- Why do you do what you do?
- What do you want to achieve?

This exercise is important because of the connections it can bring you with potential clients and businesses. When you speak to others, the initial information you share can provide them with your personality, style and approach.

what is your why and purpose for running your business?

When I started out in business, I never reviewed this exercise. I spent time networking and working with clients, but I didn't focus on what was important to me. To begin with, I didn't take the time to reflect about why I started my business in the first place.

The tools and foundations in this section will help you align your why and your purpose with the right goals and activities. These exercises will help you focus your business in the right direction and will save you time, money, and energy.

As an example, my *why* is to continue building my business to provide financial freedom for me and my family and I am passionate about supporting business owners and transforming lives through my work.

Answer these questions to understand your *why* and purpose for running your business.

- What inspires you?
- What makes you jump out of bed in the mornings?
- What would you go that extra mile for?
- What would you be doing if money was no object?

Once completed, align your *why* with your goals and vision board. Remind yourself regularly why you do what you do. Share it with your prospects, clients, and networking group. This will give them an insight into what you believe and hold valuable in your business and personally.

the accountability toolkit

For many of us, the thing we enjoy most about running our own business is being answerable only to ourselves. This can also be our biggest downfall, because without some level of external accountability, most of us let ourselves off the hook –

it's human nature. People who intentionally increase the level of accountability in their business consistently achieve more in less time.

I recommend that all my clients use the following three tools in their business to keep them personally accountable, focused and on track. You'll be astounded by the difference it makes to your results.

1. Qualifier Question

You know what it's like: you can get distracted, feel a fear of missing out, or get shiny object syndrome. Consider whether these frequent interruptions are steering you towards your goals or moving you away from them. Also, just because you are organised, that doesn't mean to say that others are. Others can step into your precious time and space because they don't have a plan or goals set.

One method you can use in your business to help you stay on track hour by hour is this qualifier question. With every challenge, distraction, interruption or shiny object, ask yourself, "Is this moving me towards my goal or moving me away from it?"

Situations with family, health, or emergencies will always happen – I am not saying for one moment that you avoid those, but concerning everything else, protect your time and boundaries.

2. Daily Planner

To keep yourself on track every single day, use a simple daily planner format. This can help focus the mind and support you with priorities to help you to achieve those daily goals.

It is important to find the groove of what is right for your process on a daily, weekly, and monthly basis. Play around with it to find when the right time for you to do your planning. Some business owners complete daily and weekly planning on a Friday, in preparation for the following week. Others plan on a Sunday for the week ahead, or on a Monday morning as the week begins. Some people find that daily planning works for them – they break down their monthly plan into daily bite-sized chunks.

Find that mode that works for you and apply it consistently to achieve ongoing results. To make the daily planner process simpler, you can download this format here:

https://links.nikimatyjasik.co.uk/accountability-toolkit

This allows you to time block your tasks and categorise them into one of three types:

- A – Urgent
- B – Important
- C – Desired

Break your tasks down further into category A, B or C to rank the priorities within each area.

3. Default Diary

It can seem a really big task to stay on track week on week and then month on month. However, when you are clear on your goals, you can work backwards to break them down into the types of activities you need to focus on. As you are probably experiencing already, when you run your business, you are everything to everyone. You're covering sales, marketing, operations, outsourcing, finance, mindset, business, and personal development. I am sure you don't need me to tell you at this stage that this is not an exhaustive list. To help you deal with this, I want to share with you the default diary. Download the simple version here:

https://links.nikimatyjasik.co.uk/accountability-toolkit

Take time out at the end of the month to see what needs to be completed for the month ahead. You can start to break down your week into regular, default activities. Perhaps you will have Money Monday, Finance Friday, Networking Tuesday, Social Media Wednesday. This will build a picture of what you need to do on a regular basis, allowing for focus, momentum, and motivation to complete the required activities. Again, this isn't set in stone: if a client needs to change around or there is an emergency, this plan can be flexed. What the default diary allows you to achieve is a focus point, a place to always refer to, and a reminder of what you need to complete to move your business forward consistently. There is that word again – *consistently*. Consistent daily action is so important. When you complete even the smallest of tasks consistently, you gain momentum.

External Accountability Measures

You can get into a consistent flow by using the tools so far: the qualifier question, the daily planner, the default diary, and the Plan, Do, Review, and Improve process. These can absolutely bring about the goals and plans you want to achieve for yourself and your business.

What about truly staying on track with your plans? You know what it's like – even the best of planners, the most highly motivated individuals can steer off track, whether it's because of mindset, imposter syndrome or fear of stepping out of their comfort zone. You can get sidetracked if no one is checking on you so I highly recommend having accountability measures in place.

You could choose the simple option of having a friend or colleague checking in with you or an option which challenges you and takes you out of your comfort zone on a higher level. All business owners should have some kind of accountability measure in place at every stage of their journey. On some occasions you could choose a mixture of things, such as a coach plus a mastermind group.

part b: moving forward with purpose

Here are a few examples of accountability you could choose from:

- Coach
- Mentor
- Business bestie
- Business buddy
- Family member or friend (I must be honest – I am not a huge fan of this option, but it can help in the early stages)
- Accountability / Masterminding group – think of it like your own board of directors
- Power groups
- Networks – connections and contacts

And even if you are exploring at this stage, always do your research. Have conversations about a range of options. Find out how they work, how they could support you, and how much it costs and over what period. You could also read the budgeting and forecasting section of this book (in *Finance*), as seeking this information in advance can help you plan where this can fit in your business and when.

Keep on track in the short term each week by using the qualifier question, the default diary, and by regularly planning each day with the daily planner.

Keep on track in the medium term with your goals and your ninety-day planner, setting aside the time for half a day each month to check in with how you are getting on and to realign any goals, activities or plans if some areas are not on course.

distractions and unexpected situations

For all the will, accountability, planning and organisation in the world, distractions and unexpected situations often throw us off track.

Here are some tried and tested tips to make sure you don't completely derail from your plans and to help you stay on track with your goals.

You can set yourself up for the day before anybody else interferes with it by starting your day with a miracle morning routine or a morning blueprint. You might do some exercise such as yoga, a walk or a run, or you might do a meditation. Even making a habit of a morning cup of herbal tea can help you stay on track that day.

You can also do this on the flipside of the day with an evening routine. You could journal about your day and write down your gratitude. This helps you to clear your head so that you do not wake up in the night thinking about lots of things in the business and you get a good night's sleep.

Time and time again, I meet business owners who don't set boundaries with their clients. They take calls and emails at any hour and become overwhelmed and frustrated that they are being contacted so often. Identify how you want to work

part b: moving forward with purpose

and what boundaries you want to set. Remember your ideal day? What time did you start and finish that day? You could also consider checking your emails only at certain times of the day and putting your 'out of office' on so that people know when to expect to hear from you, perhaps within twenty-four hours. You could have this information in your email signature.

Use call booking software like Calendly or Acuity to allow people to book their own time in your calendar. You are in control of the availability that is visible, which means you can set the boundaries in the software rather than individually with everyone in an email.

You don't have to open your whole diary. You could just say that you'll do calls Tuesday 9-12 and Thursday 12-3. The software will offer only those slots to people booking in. It also takes lots of admin off your hands.

It is important to set these boundaries. You don't want to have to answer things at any time of day across all the different communication methods that we have.

I also suggest building in some buffer hours and time at the beginning of the month so that you can provide flexibility if anything arises. When you're doing your planning for the month ahead, identify these blocks of time. Things do change each month and you need to be able to adapt the plan and have enough time to undertake the activities you need to without feeling pressured.

Look at setting boundaries with your support network, partners, family members and friends. You might have a second phone to separate work and home, and only use the work phone during certain hours. You might only give your personal number to certain people.

Sometimes emergencies can't be helped. You're always going to get situations where someone may be poorly, or something needs to be changed around. If you've got that buffer time booked in, you've always got a Plan B.

follow your plan

By creating your plan, all the foundations have been put in place to start developing your business.

It all comes together when you put your plan into action. When you work to your action plan on a daily, weekly, and monthly basis, you will be able to bring about the goals you have set within the structure of your business.

From the action plan, you can put in place a list of daily tasks to move you towards your daily, weekly, and monthly goals.

Plan, Do, Review, Improve.

When running a business, you can become caught up in the day-to-day activities and not set aside time to review.

By having an action plan (*plan*) in place to follow and implement monthly (*do*) and by setting a date at the end of each month to look back at (*review*) your activity results...

You will form the basis of the improvement (*improve*) you need to make in the month ahead when setting your next action plan.

Implementing this structured approach in your business will make it easier to set quarterly, half-yearly and yearly goals. Setting yourself a tick box chart at the beginning and end of each month will keep you on track in this area.

summary of suggested strategies to avoid distractions and deviations

- Miracle morning / evening clear routine
- Set boundaries with clients and calls and emails / details in T&Cs too.
- Expect a response within twenty-four hours if not arranged.
- Use Calendly (or similar).
- Monthly planning – build in buffer hours and time at the beginning of the month to provide flexibility if anything arises.
- Read this on a weekly basis and then on a daily basis when planning.
- Set boundaries with your support network.

- Some emergencies can't be helped so having buffer time booked in means there is a Plan B.
- Book in all client phone calls.
- Keep phone on silent and then check in regularly if call is urgent.
- Client check-ins to cover calls and any additional work for planning – being proactive rather than reactive.

summary: how to move forward in business

You now know about the qualifier question, the daily planner, and the default diary. You also know about monthly and weekly accountability to get consistent results.

Review these on a weekly basis, and it's good to set some time aside at the end of the last week of the month to plan and be clear on the next month ahead. Have a ninety-day plan in place. Working in those ninety-day blocks you can pull over that information into your monthly planning. Have clear business goals as well as clear personal goals. Focus on one at a time so that you are clear on the target you want to achieve.

Be clear on your focus so that there are no distractions. Ensure your goals are realistic and measurable, and get into the habit of writing them down every single day.

part b: moving forward with purpose

Key points quick reminder...

- Accountability (monthly)
- Always work on three months at a time
- Consider what you need for month three in the cycle
- Attach a target, a number to achieve (what's most important)
- Bring your goals over to the ninety-day plan
- Consistency
- Course correct
- Daily planner (daily)
- Default diary (weekly)
- Realistic and measurable
- Have one business goal
- Have one personal goal
- Chip away at the final goal
- Plan for support, time, and budgeting
- If you have a key goal for the year, place it in the relevant month with the date
- Qualifier question (hourly)
- Review the week
- Set aside time
- Set weekly accountability in the group
- Next month's activity
- Work in three-month (ninety-day) blocks
- Write goals down every day
- Current month activity

Hints and Tips for Weekly Planning and Accountability

None of this is new news. It is a list of questions as reminders and reference points for you to be guided to make good decisions and to be clear on what the next steps can be. They can help you see what the solutions can look like for you in your business. Always ask yourself what you have learnt, relearnt, or been reminded of.

Set that weekly space to have time to plan and review so that you're not going into the week without a plan.

Ask yourself on a weekly basis:

1. Have I planned in some business development time?
2. Am I working *on* my business rather than just working *in* it all the time?
3. Am I moving my business forward?
4. Who am I connecting with?
5. Who am I speaking to?
6. Have I blocked out time out for me?
7. How many clients am I looking to win?
8. Am I on track with my turnover and profit for the month?
9. Where am I visible to share my business this week?
10. Who is in my pipeline?
11. What support do I need around me this week in order to achieve what I need to achieve?
12. Do I have the tools and information I need to be able to do this?

part b: moving forward with purpose

13. Do I have time planned in to review my week?
14. What do my figures look like?
15. Do I know my numbers this week?
16. Am I clear on my goals?
17. Where do I need to be to improve this week?
18. Am I on track to check in with my clients' progress?
19. When will I check in with the team?
20. What are your daily qualifying questions to ensure that you're not being distracted, and you are moving towards your goal on a regular basis?

part c: managing areas of your business

sales and marketing, people, operations, finance

There is so much to learn and do when you run your own business. Every day, week, month, and year you learn something new. Everywhere you look there is a masterclass, a workshop, a webinar, or some other online training about something to do with business. It often promises to teach you the one single strategy or tactic that will skyrocket your success overnight. Hmm…

Often what happens when you take all this information in, rather than it helping you in your business, is that it leaves you feeling overwhelmed and even more aware of what you don't know enough about, or what you are not doing. And so, you do nothing with it which adds to the frustration you already feel about your business not moving forwards…

In this information age, everything you need to know and understand to grow and run a business is available for free in the public domain. The problem isn't so much that you don't know what to do, or that you don't know how to find out. The problem is that you're not *doing* it!

The following structure provides small business owners support to get this stuff done. Ultimately, that's what we get paid on – what we get *done*.

sales and marketing

When it comes to **Sales**, you can also refer to the pipeline section and review section in Part A.

I describe Sales in the following way: building relationships on a consistent basis.

Sales is a combination of all the elements of this book.

- Being clear on your message
- Being clear on your services and offering
- Listening to people – what do they really want?
- Talking to people
- Goals
- Putting in place a plan of action to connect daily with your ideal client
- Understanding the targets of your enquiries and clients

- Supporting your Sales focus with a marketing and visibility strategy

The usual area where business owners start to procrastinate is on the follow up part of sales. The focus of this sits within your pipeline and networking.

Marketing

Everyone has a different idea of what marketing is. It can cover many different areas, and every business will have a different strategy.

Visibility fits well in this section. It is my experience that when it comes to marketing and visibility you need to focus on three to five areas consistently to start seeing results.

Marketing and visibility are just as important as getting clients. Remember, you never know who is checking you out, following you and going on a journey with you through your social media. People will be working through the know, like, trust stages before they eventually book that discovery call with you or buy from you.

However, marketing and visibility tend to be the areas that business owners procrastinate on, leave to one side, and just don't implement consistently. It can be one of the last parts to be invested in and one of the first areas to be removed due to cashflow or when it's not being reviewed correctly.

When I started my business, I didn't have the budget to invest in a website or a copywriter for creating content, and social media wasn't as much of a focus point as it is now. I started by investing small and in networking and building relationships. This approach has continued to pay me back year in, year out.

So, hold on tight, because this section contains everything I can share about marketing and visibility. At the end of this, select three to five areas of visibility and marketing you want to approach. Stay committed to approaching these areas consistently to see the results. You'll have to make a note of any procrastinations around it, like money mindset, not wanting to go live on video or not wanting to ask for testimonials. Then get support on developing those areas and overcoming blocks.

Marketing and visibility are a long-term plan. You may not see the benefits for some time, but someone is always watching. We are in a world where potential clients will check us out in a number of spaces.

Right, let's get to work!

visibility strategy

This is where I start with all my clients before we even look at marketing.

To complete this properly it is important for you to be clear on:

- Your ideal client
- Where your ideal client is hanging out
- What you are passionate about in your business when it comes to visibility and strategy
- What you procrastinate on in your business when it comes to visibility and strategy
- Whether you plan to outsource; if so, to whom; what budget you have in place
- What measurements you will put in place to see what is and what isn't working
- Finally, that you commit to show up consistently with this strategy

What Do I Mean When It Comes to a Visibility Strategy?

It is important to be clear on where you are going to show up on a consistent basis, where your ideal client is hanging out and how you can reach them effectively.

Identifying where you are going to be visible every ninety days can save a lot of time, money, energy, and effort. A great benefit of working in a ninety-day cycle is that it allows time for you to review and amend the methods and strategy. It helps to keep you on track.

Visibility could be:

- Social media
- Newsletter
- Weekly email
- Social media lives
- Podcasts
- Speaking opportunities
- Networking
- Events
- Masterclasses
- Challenges and launches
- Mailshots
- Free taster sessions
- Your membership
- Lead magnets and quizzes
- Website
- Business cards
- Flyers and leaflets
- TV and radio interviews
- PR – articles in newspapers and magazines
- Free Facebook group

It's about being clear on what methods you plan to use to get your message and services out to your audience.

Take Action

Ask yourself where you want to be visible over the next ninety days. Use these questions to decide:

- Who is my ideal client?
- Where are they hanging out?
- Where do I want to be visible consistently? (Three to five areas max.)

Visibility Example:

1. Networking and speaking opportunities
2. Weekly emails and communication to my newsletter list
3. Social media – particularly Instagram

You then need to translate this into your marketing plan. To do this, you get more into the detail and ask yourself more questions:

Marketing Plan Example: (over the next ninety days)

1. Where am I networking and how many times per week?
2. How many speaking opportunities do I need and where?
3. What are the titles of my emails, what am I sharing with my audience, and what is the content?

4. Social media: which platforms, am I doing stories, lives, reels, or interviewing clients?
5. Am I planning in the time to follow the process – Plan, Do, Review, and Improve?

Top of Funnel

It is important to get clear on the types of ways people can come into your audience. Be clear on how they can access information about you so they can start to form a picture of know, like, trust. How can they form an understanding of how they can work with you to achieve their own goals?

If we can communicate clearly to our ideal client, it makes it easier for them to make decisions.

The top of your funnel could be a book, a lead magnet, a toolkit of ten top tips, running a taster session on something that you offer, offering a free invite into your membership, a workbook, an email sequence, networking, social media, an eBook that can help people in a bite-sized chunk. You might use networking or your social media stories or commenting and engaging in different Facebook groups. But whatever you choose it needs to get them into your funnel for all your offers and then communicate to your potential clients.

Having a consistent approach to the top of your funnel can help create the start of the journey for your potential clients.

After the steps above, your lead has to go somewhere next in your funnel, and this is where your systems and processes and structure can start to talk to each other to ensure you have clear communication between every touchpoint in your business.

As an example, from my accountability talk, they will automatically be entered into an email sequence and given the opportunity to join my free Facebook group. They will be given the opportunity to have an offer on my digital workbook which they can download at a reduced price (this is called a tripwire).

They will also have access to book a call with me. This process leads them to easy touchpoints in my business where I can start to build know, like, trust. They will start to receive weekly emails from me along with the option to connect on social media platforms and join the waitlist for any events I have coming up.

Another option which can get great results is having a quiz as a lead magnet. This gives the recipient an instant answer and they can link easily to the next step of what you offer.

Build the funnel you create into your review so you start to really see where and how your funnel creates the enquiries.

networking

The Power of Your Network

Networking is one of the easiest and most effective ways to build those close relationships with like-minded business owners.

It helps you to stay on track with building those relationships and getting referrals, recommendations, and the word-of-mouth recognition that you are looking for.

If you're not networking already and you'd like to do so, here are my top tips on what to do to get started:

- Research in advance – what is available to you.
- Attend a selection of meetings to see if they are suitable.
- Try online sessions and in-person sessions. Perhaps a mix of the two will suit you best.
- Check if your ideal client is hanging out in the room.
- Be prepared with your sixty seconds and with how people can connect with you.
- Be clear on why you would like to join a networking group; what's the purpose of it?
- Seek recommendations from fellow business owners to see where they are networking and how beneficial they find it.
- Networking can happen at breakfast, at lunch or during the evening. Choose what's right for you.

- Once you have decided on a group, check in with your budgets (more on that later) and put all the meeting dates and any one-to-ones for the next ninety days in your planner.
- Stick to a particular group or set of groups to build that trust and relationship. This helps build a support network that you can rely on.
- Being in front of that group will help build your confidence, your messaging, and your presenting skills.

I recommend having ideally one day a month when you are carrying out your networking and one-to-ones on a set day (use the default diary for this).

Your sixty seconds needs to be memorable, clear and to stand out as there are lots of people in network meetings and lots to digest and take on board. You want people to leave with a clear understanding of the types of clients you are looking for and your ideal audience. If you can, ask for a specific referral to a particular person or company.

Sixty-second exercise:

1. Your name and your business name
2. What you do
3. A strapline that guides people to understand what you do
4. Keywords to help people pinpoint and listen

5. Explain how you help your clients
6. What they say about you
7. What you are looking for
8. And finish by repeating points one and three

It is fine to read out your sixty seconds, and to use the same one several times. This will help your regular networking audience to listen and get familiar with you. People pick up information at different speeds. Repetition of your sixty seconds on a regular basis means that it will stay in their minds.

When it comes to networking, be consistent. You have to keep going with it – and if you do, it will bring about the results you're looking for. Sometimes you'll become very busy, but you have to keep showing up consistently. Meeting people will give you a boost, too.

When you're at a networking meeting, take good notes. Write down the key things that others share with you and think about whether it would be easy for you to start referring them to people you know – that's good networking.

Identify which people in the room you would like to have a one-to-one with. First think about the members, then the visiting members, and then the guests. It is important to build relationships with everyone: you don't know who people know!

One-to-ones

The next step is to set a target around the number of one-to-ones you would like to have every week and every month. Initially, start planning them in within your ninety-day plan. Decide how many one-to-ones you would like to have in your schedule and book them in using Calendly (or your preferred alternative). Keep them to an allocated time with a maximum of thirty minutes for an initial one-to-one.

Spend those thirty minutes getting to know each other's business. Ask them key questions about their business and their plans for the future. Ask useful questions which allow you to understand how the other person could support your clients. Don't wait to be referred by others; start referring them and this will be remembered.

Share all your social media pages and handles and take note of the other person's too. Follow up with the other person so they know how you are getting on and vice versa. Hold your nerve while waiting for results to happen. By being consistent in your activity you will create momentum that leads to results.

Testimonials

This falls into marketing as well as the operational process, and it is important to get into the habit of asking clients for testimonials during and after any experience with you.

Below are sample questions you could ask your clients to get the best out of a testimonial from them and to make it suit what you want to use it for.

- What was the situation that led to you taking this service... joining this membership... etc?
- Please describe the experience of the service you received.
- Please outline the benefits and results you have enjoyed from working with me.
- What value has this service brought to you and what will you take forward in your business?
- What would you say to someone else considering this type of service?

You may want your client to produce written or video testimonial; you might want to get bite-sized chunks and words from them so that you can use them within your marketing. Once you have the testimonials, you can plan in accordingly to make sure that the testimonial fits in the right space of what you're launching and when you're launching.

Speaking

When you are ready in your business to share your message, your business, your service, and your story with confidence and clarity, then you are ready to speak to an audience.

This can be done in several ways:

- Being interviewed on a podcast
- In a member slot or keynote speaking slot at a network meeting
- Your sixty seconds at a networking meeting
- Running a master class on a certain topic
- Speaking in mastermind groups or memberships
- Being on stage in front of a bigger audience

These can either be paid or unpaid opportunities, but the value comes from them being great ways to raise your visibility, get your message out there, and to help people understand who you are and what you do.

Social Media

When I started out, I didn't use social media in my business.

For the first five years I built my entire business on word of mouth, recommendation, and referrals. That was through the networking methods that you have just read. However, social media provide such great spaces where we can be visible to a much wider audience than in face-to-face networking.

It's important to understand what platforms you personally want to hang out on.

And then it's crucial, when you look at that visibility strategy, to understand where your ideal client is hanging out and how you can connect with them. Alongside that, you can use things like stories, reels, and lives. There are so many ways. You can use various methods to communicate to your audience but finding what is right for you must be a personal preference. The key consideration is that you get a consistent message out there and are able to engage and share comments and information further with your clients.

The social media platform and the way you use it must connect with you. You have to feel passionate about it and if you find that you're procrastinating on this, then it is helpful to have somebody who can help you with a content marketing plan and strategy for your social media. When you start to get into hashtags, keywords, photos, and the right imagery for you to use, it can be quite time consuming. However, approached in the right way it can be beneficial to raise your profile within your industry and in front of your ideal clients.

PR

To a lot of people PR means things like being in the papers but that's not all that it's about. This is about finding spaces where you can share your message with your ideal clients through articles in your chosen publications.

You could be communicating with existing clients or finding a new audience. There are lots and lots of different methods. You could do this through articles in magazines or newspapers, or by being featured on TV or a radio channel in an interview. If you choose this as part of your visibility strategy it could help you get to that much wider audience. You could use this to raise your profile in an ongoing way throughout the year or around certain services that you're launching or certain messages that you want to get out there at given times.

Being prepared for PR is having:

- A clear bio
- The right photos
- The right message
- Topics you can talk about

Connection and Collaboration

Connection and collaboration can form part of (and be a major benefit of) the networking structure that you adopt. When you network you can look for those key connections that have a real synergy with you, your business, your message, your vision, your goals and where you plan to go with your business. Then you can form collaborations with people and businesses that are strongly supportive of that message.

It is important to set clear boundaries within these collaborations, to understand where the strategy is, and to know how you can complement each other to deliver an offer. Normally a collaboration is not a paid option until you get paying clients, so it is crucial to set the boundaries and have each person show up to deliver their part of the collaboration in an effective way. You save time, money, and energy when you have the right method and process in place for each collaborative partner.

Blogs, Newsletters and Emails

These work well for a lot of businesses. Regular blogs or case studies on chosen methods or topics in your business can allow you to communicate how you may respond to a particular enquiry, how you may deliver a service, or how you support clients. When you have a case study, you are recounting an actual live example of how you have supported a client, how you've taken them on a journey, and how you have built the relationship with them and helped them to work forward.

Newsletters and weekly emails are a great method for communicating with your audience that don't hang out on social media and don't go to networking. Often, they like to read something in a lot more detail so sending out regular newsletters and emails to communicate the message from the week can be a great way to approach that audience.

Knowing Your Competitors

It helps to know who offers the same or similar service to you, even if it's not a direct comparison. Get an idea of who's offering what, how they are communicating it, how they are speaking to their ideal clients, how much they may be charging, what their offers and services are, and what top of funnel options they use for their clients. Don't copy what they do but do get an insight. We are all individuals and people buy people, but knowing your competitors means you can provide your niche and have your own identity. There are enough clients to go around for everyone.

Do I Need a Website?

I spent the first five years of my business with no website. It is only recently that I have launched a website into my marketing and visibility strategy and plan.

When you start out in your business and are trying to communicate your message (or even if you have been in business for a little while), you ask yourself:

- Do I really need a website at this stage?
- Do I need to invest in a website?
- What other options and methods to share my message are available to me?
- How costly will a website be?
- How much time is it going to take up?
- Is a website really going to serve me in my business journey right now?

After asking these questions, consider that when it comes to websites and branding it takes time, energy, and effort. It can be a distraction from planning and getting consistency in the business.

Marketing Summary

When setting your marketing plan and budget, it is important to be clear on the following areas to ensure that the marketing plan works for you and your business.

You can be bombarded with lots of suggestions on how to get your message to market, but it must fit with you. If your marketing has scored low in your business until now, here is an action plan for how to tackle it. Build the activities into your Plan, Do, Review, and Improve process that you created using Part A of this book.

- Make a list of the marketing areas you feel would benefit your business.
- Research each of these areas, including how they benefit your business.
- Set a budget against each of the marketing areas you decide to move forward with.
- What support do you need to bring this plan to life?
- What structures are available to you to build and implement a plan?
- What social media platforms do you plan to use?
- Where do you start with social media advertising and presence for your business?

Once you are established with your initial plan, consider where other areas of marketing can fit within your business:

- Branding – what are my colours, themes, image, and message to my audience?
- Website – do I need a website for my business? What can this give me that I don't get from social media?
- Photography – do I need professional shots to promote my business to my audience.
- Affiliates – will you work with other businesses to promote their services?
- Referral Plan – will you use this once you are established with a client database?
- Business Materials – business cards, leaflets, postcards, banners.
- Testimonials – asking your clients for a testimonial to build messages to use in your marketing.

people

Outsourcing

When it comes to outsourcing, take your time to decide what fits right for you and your budget. Time and time again I have seen business owners become way too busy and overwhelmed and dive straight into finding a PA, VA, social media resource and don't know what they are going to give them. If you follow this simple method detailed below, you will save yourself time, money, energy, and a lot of frustration.

Over a Two-to-Four-Week Period…

- Complete the daily planner every day. At the end of each day review the tasks/activities you have completed. Alongside it, add how long it took you to complete. Also add whether you need to complete this task yourself in the future or whether you can give it to someone else.
- Complete the default diary. At the end of each week review it and ask yourself whether you are completing the tasks and allocating enough time to the tasks. Also ask whether you love completing these parts of your business or are they a procrastination?
- At the end of the month review, ask what has worked well and what can be improved upon.
- Along with your research, recommendations, conversations you've had, and your understanding of time and cost, you will be in a much better place to plan in who you need, when you need them, and you will be ready to go with a list of actions.

operations

Operations in your business covers systems, processes, and structure. It is the procedures you have in place to run your business with efficiencies and ease and helps you provide the best possible experience to your client.

Systems and Processes

Here are some examples of how you might run projects on certain systems or processes within your business. There are so many to access, so much that you can use daily to communicate with your team and with your audience.

These are just a few suggestions of what you can use. I would recommend making a note of what the process is, what you need it to do, and how much interaction that process needs – is it manual, is it automated? Start to ask questions of what you want that part of the process to look like so you can determine the right tool to help you deliver.

Ideas:

- Asana – project management board
- Trello – project management board
- Mighty Hubs to monitor progress of a project
- Communication tools – Voxer, WhatsApp, Facebook group, Facebook Messenger, Instagram messenger, Instagram group, LinkedIn message, LinkedIn group, Slack
- Calendly, Acuity, Kartra, Kajabi – scheduling and membership sites

Identify what needs to be addressed in your business and then seek recommendations and referrals on types of software and apps that can be used to address that problem. Alternatively, find a tech VA, or an Operations Manager or

Online Business Manager who can help you to not only identify the right processor model but also to do the set-up for you.

As with any chosen process, you need to implement it, test it, and ensure it's doing everything you need it to do in your business. You may be using it individually or you may need to roll it out to your team and have their involvement as well.

Development of Your Systems and Processes – What Next?

Systems and processes evolve over time. Everyone starts off with manual processes, using spreadsheets, Word, a notebook and pen, and manual ways of collecting information in the first instance. Regardless of whether you're at the beginning of your business or five-plus years, it's important to identify what you need at each stage.

I speak from experience here. My business has grown and developed, yet my systems and processes and structure have not always been strong enough to support that growth. By reviewing every ninety days, based on the number of clients you have and the price points and packages that you're charging, you can decide whether you need to outsource, whether you still need a manual process, or whether you can start to move to an automated process.

Mapping out your process can also be useful to help you identify all the touchpoints of your clients or prospective clients. (Covered in Marketing section.)

Once a client has converted, Operations relates to how easy it is for us or our team to look after them. We need to have touchpoints every step of the way to give them the support, the information, and the next steps that they need.

Examples from my own business:

- A client that starts with me either one-to-one, in a masterminding group, or in a membership will receive a welcome email, a thank you card, and a welcome gift.
- We address how they are communicated with – a one-to-one client receives a workbook, communications initially via email and if required we set up a Trello board; they can have access to me and they can update me in a really easy way.
- When it comes to masterminding groups, we use Trello or Karta to communicate on a regular basis about trainings, the central diary, and updates with information that needs to be downloaded for reviewing.

Form a process within every service offered. Ask yourself:

- How do I communicate with that client?
- How do I collect the information about the client?
- Where do I have that information about my client stored so that they and I can access it with ease?

- What tools do they need to get the most from the service?

All this determines what a successful relationship looks like. It takes time to embed. Having somebody to support from a technical operational side eventually in your business as you're growing and developing can be really helpful.

When you have had that successful working journey with your client and you're coming to the end of your time together, having good aftersales care is important so they can either understand where they can access you again or they can leave with a great experience and can refer you to others. I have several clients who work with me for a block of time, then go away and implement what they need to do, and then come back and work with me again. That is all down to me communicating with them on a regular basis. I will include a thank you note or thank you gift. I'll make sure they're on my email list, social media platforms so we stay connected, along with networking groups to check in.

Even if that client is in one of your networking groups or networking spaces, you should still stay connected on a regular basis through your aftersales care. Have those touchpoints and be clear on your pipeline follow up. That client could go into your CRM system for you to touch base and say hello in three to six months' time. You could ask how their progress is going: what's working, what's not working and how they are getting on with implementing the work you did together.

That leads nicely on to the importance of your CRM (pipeline) system.

Managing Your Pipeline

Managing your pipeline needs to be one of the key priorities in your business. Below, I have captured a checklist that you can use on a regular basis to manage your pipeline effectively.

First, identify a system that you can have in place to manage your pipeline daily. It's important to be able to touch your pipeline every single day.

Look to have a structure to manage your pipeline, such as a spreadsheet by month or a CRM system (customer record management system) which can be automated, such as Asana, Trello, or Capsule.

Another system is to simply use email folders to keep all your pipeline stored. Remember, communicate monthly with everyone in your pipeline. Whether they are interested in your business or have an enquiry about a service, a course, or an offering you've got coming up, every single person should be in your pipeline.

Every single person you speak to is initially a prospect. You never know when you might connect with them and you never know when they might be referring someone else to you, because ultimately you don't know where this conversation is going to lead. It can take between six and eight weeks from initial enquiry and connection all the way through to a conversion. It can now take on average up to twenty-seven touchpoints for somebody to see you and your business to build the know, like, trust factor.

Everyone in your pipeline should have a next step, even if that is just sending them an email to summarise your conversation, sending them your offers with your links or emailing them with a quote. It could even be to say that it was great to catch up and you'd love to catch up again in a few months' time to see where they are at in their business.

Adopting this process helps you to build relationships and build consistency month in and month out, and to cover any gaps that you might experience in your business – it helps to cover those peaks and troughs. With this approach you have a consistent flow of enquiries, and you end up being front of mind for people.

Be clear on the touchpoints you plan to have in place. This could relate to the earlier section about your visibility strategy.

Other methods could be:

- Using the DMs (direct messaging)
- Emailing
- Sending a thank you card or a note in the post
- Voice note

- Or the old-fashioned way – give them a call!

From this, confirm which touchpoints you will use once the initial connection has been formed.

I identify keen enquiries in my pipeline as my 'hotties'. These people are ready to go with deciding and are quite a warm lead. They might be gathering more information before deciding to work with me, or they are just ready to go! I also have those that are not ready right now and can sit in my pipeline for a follow up in three to six months' time.

Have the flow and strategy in place because no one is a no forever; no just means they're not ready right now in terms of time or investment. They will be ready when they are ready and by nurturing that sequence and your audience it can feel effortless.

Pipeline is certainly an area where a lot of business owners do procrastinate, so it's important to find a method that works for you, and that you can touch on every single day to connect with just one or two people and follow up with one or two people.

When you speak with someone who has made an enquiry, make good notes. They will feel a connection through you saying things like, "Did you have a nice weekend?" or "I remember you said you liked surfing/champagne/chocolate," or I remember you said it was your husband's fiftieth." Whatever it may be, people will remember that you remembered those things and it will stand out.

Identifying your contact's preferred communication method is a key golden nugget of information and can just save so much time. If you are talking to somebody and you email them, they might not check their emails for a week. They might be someone who just doesn't enjoy email, but if you ask them when you're speaking to them, "What's your preferred method of communication?" you can get a real steer as to what they will respond most quickly to. It could be Facebook Messenger, WhatsApp, text, email, Instagram, LinkedIn. Monitor where and when you get your quickest responses from clients.

Following on from the networking section earlier, when you get leads and enquiries coming into your business they can come in from a few different pathways. Start getting clear on how you begin to capture leads and enquiries. As you've seen in the visibility and marketing section, you can end up communicating in so many ways. This may be through word-of-mouth recommendation or referral, or through Facebook, Instagram, LinkedIn, or through your website – there is a whole host of pathways along which you can start to receive these leads and enquiries. Knowing in your business which pathways are most frequently used can help you direct your efforts.

Start a spreadsheet to collate what these leads and enquiries look like and where they are from, getting as much information down as possible with regards to that lead. Respond to the lead by asking them for a call by phone or Zoom, because then you can ask the right questions, hear more about them and gauge their personality, and determine whether you are a good fit and you're able to help them.

With the information and with the process that you use in order to help that client, once the call is over, summarise the conversation and what has been agreed in an email, whether it's a quote or some information that needs to be sent out. Then the next steps are put into motion.

You can map this out on a flow chart:

1. The enquiry.
2. The phone or zoom call.
3. Collate in your spreadsheet where the enquiry came from
4. How does this link to your marketing and visibility strategy?
5. What is and what isn't working in this part of the strategy?
6. Summarise the call in an email.
7. Arrange a follow up within twenty-four hours, even if this is a quick text or WhatsApp so that you can find out if they have received the information that you sent.
8. Understand their best method of communication.

9. Move them into your pipeline process. Have a space where you can monitor your pipeline process.

When somebody recommends you or makes a referral to you and that converts into a paying client, it is a good idea to recognise the person who made the recommendation or referral. That could be with a thank you card or a gift as a gesture of gratitude, to really say thank you for referring that person. It is also a thank you to them for their acknowledgement that you are really good at what you do.

Start referring and recommending people into businesses in your network *before* you begin receiving them yourself. This can really help you to stand out in the eyes of others because you are building the principles of know, like, and trust. They see that you have paid attention and you understand what they do. You might have used their services yourself, or you might have heard first-hand from their clients how amazing they are so you know that they are a solid referral.

Checklist for managing your pipeline.

- System in place to manage daily
- Spreadsheet by month, CRM, or email
- Everyone should be on your pipeline: every one-to-one, every enquiry, every business conversation
- You don't know where a connection is going to lead
- Touch your pipeline every day to keep updated
- Everyone in your pipeline should have a next step

- Build relationships and consistency
- What touchpoints do you have in place?
- Is this mapped out e.g., social media, follow up to a one-to-one, information sent out because of an enquiry?
- Who in your pipeline are 'hotties'?
- Who in your pipeline are information gathering and will need a follow up?
- Who needs a follow up in a few months to check in?
- Pipeline doesn't feel overwhelming – move to a certain month or put a follow-up date

Your takeaway from this section is the importance of having a clear customer journey, the systems and processes, and the aftercare in place in your business. Map it out and do not miss a step.

If you would prefer to gain expert support when it comes to your customer journey, processes and your CRM, my answer is to speak to Sarah Newland of keyboardsmash.net. Sarah is amazing and she absolutely knows her stuff.

Processes and Procedures

You might have an NDA (non-disclosure agreement) in place when working with freelancers, or you might have a confidentiality agreement or ask them for their terms and conditions.

It is important as well to have your own terms and conditions when you work with clients, which you should try to keep as simple as possible. I recommend, depending on what the document is, that you get legal advice. I also recommend that your terms and conditions vary slightly between your different offerings. For example, the terms and conditions for my masterminding groups are slightly different from those for my one-to-one work and my membership. Bear in mind what the differentials need to be so that you can tweak accordingly.

When it comes to policies and procedures in your business, you may want to document how a certain system, process or structure runs so that you can outsource that with ease to somebody else. You can capture this in a Word document, on Trello or on Asana somewhere it's easy to access. If you're considering taking on employees within your business, then you are required to speak with an HR professional and a legal perspective so sourcing that kind of expertise and advice will help determine the types of policies and procedures that you need in place in order to cover any eventuality in your business and to protect yourself and your business when hiring.

finance

Touch Your Business Numbers Every Day

I remember in the early days of my business that someone asked me how I kept on top of all the numbers and the pipeline in my business.

My very simple answer was I touched these details every single day and looked at my business numbers, my bank accounts, and my pipeline daily to help me really understand the position I was in. I found it was important to do this because in the early days I was fearful of looking at these types of numbers. I know numbers aren't everybody's favourite thing, but they help you keep a steer on what is going on with enquiries, conversions, money in and money out. You can check in daily with every single type of number in your business. There might not be a huge amount of movement, but even that might be the indication you need that you should be doing more activity to be bringing more of those numbers in. Your numbers can always tell you a daily story.

The Numbers

Numbers is the area that a lot of business owners ignore, procrastinate on, or just don't want to look at. What I'm going to take you through are some clear and easy hints and tips to consider when you are looking at the numbers in your business. Forming a good relationship with a great accountant and bookkeeper can really help. This saves so much in terms of time, energy, money, understanding and clarity. It's beneficial to have this in place if you find yourself completely ignoring this part of your business.

Accounts

Being on track with your accounts month on month is so beneficial. Time and time again I see clients or business owners submitting their accounts at the very last minute. They have a real rush and race to the finish line by the deadline. I've been there too. I've done this several times before and it has cost me dearly every single time. As soon as you can in your business, I urge you to find a great accountant and bookkeeper. The process can help you stay on track with this on a monthly basis.

As your business grows and develops, I recommend having a ninety-day planning session in place with your accountant to help you understand the following:

- Your numbers
- Your profit
- What's working and what's not working
- Where you could be spending too much money
- Where you could be saving money
- Forecasting so that you know where you can invest
- What the business is going to look like when it comes to becoming a limited company or on the VAT threshold

- How much tax you've got to pay so you can set aside the right amount of money on a regular basis to hit the deadline of paying it to HMRC

Pricing and Packages

Schedule to review your pricing and packages in your business every six months. Be clear on your ideal client, your marketing and visibility and where your ideal client hangs out. I would also review your competitors so you can really identify what you are doing versus what you're planning to do. You could consider having focus groups or gaining feedback from your current clients? You could look at testimonials to see what's really working and where people are getting results. It can help you to determine the right pricing and packaging.

If you have any limiting beliefs or money blocks around your pricing, I encourage you to seek out a coach or mentor or a sounding board to help you work through this. I can highly recommend Denise Duffield Thomas's book *Get Rich, Lucky Bitch* or Fanny Snaith, Certified Money Coach so you can identify where your blocks are and how to overcome them.

Budgets and Forecasting

This exercise ties in with your ninety-day planning and your numbers.

It is so important to have your budgeting and forecasting in place as you could be making decisions to spend money within your business without considering whether you are profitable, whether you actually need certain things in your business, or whether you've got time to take those things on board and implement them.

Consider what you need to budget into your expenditure in order to achieve your goals in your ninety-day plan and link it to be where you want to be with your year-end goal.

What do you need to forecast in your numbers based on the activity levels and the types and number of clients that you need to get there? This can be broken down simply into money in and money out, then overlay that with the number of clients per service and offer that you would like to work with. You can then be clear on your available cashflow in the business – how much do you want to spend in set areas of your business?

Managing Finances

These are further elements that you can set into your ninety-day plan and default diary.

Manage your finances on a regular basis to ensure that you are paying things on a set day, for example. You can focus on what has come in, what you're paying out, and you can then focus on what else you could potentially do to bring more money in.

- Look at the cash flow.
- Invoice at the right time.

- Be clear with the terms and conditions.
- Budget and forecast accordingly.
- Look at the costs and expenditure analysis to make sure that the business is running as effectively as possible.
- Start with the ninety-day period, then break it back down into monthly, weekly and daily periods.

Invoicing

I recommend having an invoicing system in place such as Xero or QuickBooks. This is a tool which lets you utilise an automated function to send your invoicing and notifications out. Invoicing can be done throughout the month, at the beginning of the month or the end of the month – whenever suits your services and your terms and conditions. Bringing it into your process helps you to understand what fits and works well for you and helps you to identify what you need to do to achieve good cash flow, such as when you should be invoicing, what terms you should be offering, whether you ask for payment immediately, or in seven, fourteen or thirty days. I don't recommend small business owners offer any more than thirty days. A lot of businesses ask for payment ahead of any session or service provided and this means that the time, service or offering is secured for the client and secured for you.

Cost Analysis

Bring into your ninety-day planning a cost analysis of all your time, services and offerings that you provide to ensure that they are continuing to be profitable and effective. Look at different ways that you might save costs. You might be over-paying for something, not getting the right service, or you may find that you are just spending too much money in one certain area. You might be able to reduce or condense your costs. Building this into your ninety-day planning will really be effective to make sure you're on track with working out what you are spending and why.

How Much Does Your Debt Cost?

When I started out in my business, I was some £50,000 pounds in debt, and I didn't want to look at it for a long time. I was too ashamed, too fearful, and felt very uncomfortable with looking at the real true facts of my debt situation. When the pain point was too much, I sought guidance and advice to help me to work through it.

This could be blocking you from moving forward. If that is you and if this is your situation, work through how you can face up to that debt sooner rather than later. Work to find a way that you can build your business in order to start clearing that debt.

Check your credit file and seek out advice, maybe from a mortgage advisor or an independent financial advisor to understand all your options at the initial stages. My story really transformed once I got my head around what my debt was costing me on a monthly basis and what I had to do in my business to help me grow to the levels that I needed to in order to clear the debt. You really can achieve it if you set your mind to it.

Business Model

Cost, quantity, and growth form around your business planning and business activity and what you have in place for your year-end goal and your ninety-day planning.

Having a business model in place helps you look at your:

- Planning
- Structure
- Marketing and visibility
- Budgets and annual forecasts
- Semi-passive income and passive income
- Outsourcing to a team
- Services and offerings that you want to make sure are in your plan
- Balance in your business – aligned with the elements of the Plan, Do, Review, and Improve section
- Review of your number section – to help you get the cost, the quality, the quantity and the growth in place
- Time and capacity
- Pricing

Finance Summary

You might think that this is a bit old school, and there are lots of options out there, but I still use a cash book, a gratitude income book, and a spreadsheet to track all my income. Then I move on to using QuickBooks. I check against that system and view the relevant reports to see if I'm on track with everything, then check in with my accountant. My activity in a number of these areas is thanks to the amazing book by Denise Duffield Thomas. Track gratitude in a notebook for each one that comes into you, whether that's a client paying, you've had a discount, or a client has bought you a coffee, taken you out for lunch, bought you flowers, or you've had a saving on something. Detail each one that you have received in your business and in your life, no matter what it is.

When you track everything, whether it is income related or related to saving money, you can really start to tot up how much money is coming into you, how much money you might be saving, and how many things are gifted to you. You're ultimately saving that money, which is really impactful and powerful.

Physically writing down what comes into my business and what goes out of my business, as well as what comes into me personally and what goes out personally, helps me resonate with how much money I could be receiving and how much money I could be spending. You might find it a little time consuming to begin with, but it actually doesn't take up a huge amount of time on a regular basis. It is a simple strategy to be on top of your numbers every single day.

To align with the Plan, Do, Review, and Improve structure, simply score your business out of ten, in the four key areas of Sales and Marketing, People, Operations and Finance.

Where do you score each time? What is your lowest score?

Ask yourself what is really going on for you in this area of your business.

Align the score to the section of the book to help find the next steps.

Examples to help when scoring:

Sales and Marketing

Do you have a plan? Are you converting the leads you want? Are you creating the enquiries you want? Do you have a consistent marketing and visibility strategy?

People

Who is around you that can either be helping or hindering the progression in your business? Is it you? Friends, family, clients, suppliers, your network?

Operations

Your systems, processes, structure, and procedures. What do you have in place to run your business smoothly and create a great customer experience?

Finance

Your cashflow, money in the bank, pricing, buffer pot, payment terms. Are you satisfied with the turnover and profit consistently in your business?

Frequently Asked Questions

Below is a selection of frequently asked business questions. If a question sounds familiar, or it represents a problematic area for you in your business, take the question and seek out the initial next step with the appropriate section(s) of the book. You will find that each question fits into one of the categories of Sales and Marketing, People, Operations, or Finance, or they could fit over a few.

How do I understand who the audience for my new offer is? **(Sales and Marketing)**

How do I get the best out of my day to maximise my income? **(Operations and Finance)**

How do I track my numbers effectively and on a consistent basis, to give me financial security? **(Operations and Finance)**

How do I present myself to get the clients I want? **(Sales and Marketing and People)**

How do I manage my time effectively between now and the next meeting to implement my massive to-do list? **(Operations)**

How do I create the right marketing strategy to kick off conversations with corporates? **(Sales and Marketing)**

How do I maximise the opportunities from my new website? **(Sales and Marketing)**

How do I select the right networking for my business and implement it effectively to gain clients? **(Sales and Marketing)**

How do I know what I am good at so that I can deliver effectively into my business? **(People)**

How do I reach my ideal client effectively and with the right content to create, engage and build relationships? **(Sales and Marketing)**

How do I make a harmonious team, as well as run an organised business? **(People and Operations)**

How do I overcome my block to formulate my online course? **(People)**

How do I get clarity on what is blocking me in my business? **(People)**

How do I bring more leads into my pipeline? **(Sales and Marketing and Operations)**

How do I develop systems and actions to build my FB group audience consistently? **(Sales and Marketing and Operations)**

How do I decide on the right systems and processes to deliver my business model effectively? **(Operations)**

How do I pull together and implement my FB group, freebie, breadcrumbs and email sequence within a month? **(Sales and Marketing)**

How do I reconnect with my client base and prospects to build relationships and confidence? **(Sales and Marketing)**

How do I approach a sales and marketing process strategy that suits me and my personality? **(Sales and Marketing and People)**

How do I manage my business life better? **(People and Operations)**

How do I create semi-passive and passive income into my business? **(Sales and Marketing and Operations)**

How do I get out of my own way? **(People)**

How do I manage my business time more effectively to get through the overwhelm? **(Operations)**

How do I get in front of the right prospects? **(Sales and Marketing)**

How do I keep the momentum and focus with the changes in my business to provide results and consistency? **(People)**

How do I stop trading time for money? **(Finance and Operations)**

How do I get out of my own way to charge the right amount? **(People and Finance)**

How do I make strong and smarter decisions in my business to achieve strong profits consistently of £10k per month? **(People and Finance)**

How do I create consistent enquiries and a pipeline to build clients for my main service? **(Sales and Marketing)**

How do I set clear boundaries with myself and my clients? **(Operations and People)**

How do I engage with my audience consistently through LinkedIn and Instagram to create conversation? **(Sales and Marketing)**

How do I streamline my enquiry to conversion process to gain a more consistent flow of clients? **(Operations)**

How do I develop a future for my business? **(Finance and Sales and Marketing)**

How do I manage my time effectively between two businesses? **(Operations)**

How do I develop my retainer offering in my business to achieve an additional £1000 per month? **(Finance)**

How do I balance the books at the end of each month to cover my investment? **(Finance)**

part d: a-z business guide

This is your go-to space to get an initial insight or decision on a certain challenge, question, or solution in your business. You face so many questions as a business owner, and a lot of the time you just need that piece of information to spark what you probably already know. From this space you will either learn, relearn, or be reminded of a next step you can take, saving you time, money, effort, and energy.

***

A =

Accountability

This for sure is the area (apart from people asking me how they get more clients) that business owners flounder on. Having great accountability measures in place can be the real key area in your business where you are lacking the support that you need. If that is you, have a look at:

- What accountability measures do you have in place?
- Has this book helped you identify the accountability measures that are possible?
- How can you go and find them and then put them in place consistently to see the results?
- What support, encouragement and changes do you need to see for yourself?

Keep on track

The accountability measures in place to keep us on track could be a coach, a mentor, a business bestie, a business buddy, a networking buddy, or a masterminding group.

Affiliates

To contribute towards your financial goal, you may have elements in your business plan and business setup which allow you to link as an affiliate to a course, membership, system, or process that you use. Being set up with a link that you can share with others to create a commission for yourself can be a great semi-passive income.

Affirmations

Have daily affirmations that form a place that supports you to be aligned with your goals, your vision, with what's important to you and with what you want to focus on and where you want to be. Saying these regularly can help to bring about what you want to focus on, what you believe in, and ultimately what you want to manifest and make happen. Here are a few examples of what those could be on a daily basis. You can take some time to reflect on what's important to you and what you want to be saying to yourself:

- I am my own superhero
- I am strong
- I can do this
- I believe in myself
- I am doing this

Taking *Action*

I'm going to simply call this JFDI (just f*****g do it!).

It's important to take action. You can procrastinate, you can overthink things, you can think the worst and that it's not going to work out, you can worry that it's not going to go to plan, but actually a lot of the time it's just about taking that leap of faith. It is about holding your nerve and taking the action to see what comes about. It's about getting on with it, not waiting for perfection, not procrastinating, just getting the ninety-day plan in place, and learning from it. You may lack confidence or clarity in what you're doing to begin with, but until you do the actions and until you get the results, you don't know what it looks like.

B =

Buffer – **Plan (clients and development)**

When planning client and business development time in your business, I believe that you need to be in a space of having 80% business clients and serving those clients and then look to have 20% capacity for business development and space to be flexible. It gives you a buffer to be able to run at a pretty good pace rather than overwhelming yourself, and it can give you good guidance to not say yes to everything so that you can actually have some time and space to work on your business *and* have some downtime.

Boundaries - **Set boundaries between your work and life**

This one really went to pot for many people during the pandemic. Time and time again I saw that business owners were spending so much time on their business and their work that there were no boundaries in place with life. Where did one stop and the other start? So many business owners have been predominantly working from home, particularly over the last two to three years, and don't have that space to be able to move away from work, or into a creative, clear space to work on themselves and their business.

Be clear of your boundaries to have that clear divide between work and life so that they are not crossing over. You must be strict with yourself.

I understand that it is hard to ensure that there's no crossover. It is learned over a period of time. You need to work out what is right for you but to speak from experience, by having an office I spend very little time on my laptop or in meetings when I'm at home. This is my downtime and home is where I spend time with my family.

Boundaries - **Avoid people who drain your time**

There is nothing to say here other than to avoid negative people as much as you can. We all experience them; there are lots of people with opinions, who say you should do it like this, you should do it like that, when they don't have any experience of what you're doing. At times they will share how, in their opinion, they would even actually do it. It is normal for people to act in this way and quite simply, it's down to the fact that they would love to be doing what you're doing. However, they don't have the gumption to do it or to want to step out of their comfort zone. Try as much as you can to avoid people who drain your energy. It's challenging to begin with, but it is very refreshing once you set those boundaries and decide to switch off from those types of people.

* * *

C =

***Community* - Business can be isolating**

It can be lonely to run a business. You can feel isolated. However, there are many ways that we can be connected to likeminded business owners. This can be through networking, coaching, mastermind groups, finding business besties or having your business buddies in place. It is important to find people you can talk to so that you don't feel like you are just running your business solo. You can run your business with support around you. You can have sounding boards to turn to when you need to.

Ask yourself whether you are feeling isolated. If you are new to business, you might not yet have people around you who understand what you're doing. How can you put a support network in place for yourself? Where can you hang out? Do you prefer to meet people in person or online? Which is more important to you?

***Client* Database**

A client database is important for you to build the foundations of your business. It is the central hub for so many parts of your business and you save time by having a database. Refer to the operations section to read about the many CRM systems available to build an information database. It is important to find the system that works for you and your business requirements. Don't forget that a simple spreadsheet can be a great start pointing to capture all of this.

Capturing Information and Data

Ask yourself these questions:

1. Who are you going to speak to about your business and your services?
2. Who are you going to share your story with?
3. How are you going to capture their details?
4. What data do you need to capture on a regular basis?
5. Where are your financials, social media stats, website stats, conversion rates?
6. What format is the data in?
7. What data do you need to capture monthly?
8. How do you capture what's working and not working to see what's right for you?

Refer to both the Operations and Pipeline sections to add more detail to these areas.

Collaborations

Once your one-to-one follow-up process is established and your reputation is building within your chosen market and marketing strategy, collaborations can work well. Adopting this approach can also give your business a team to draw on when your business grows.

Hints and tips on how this can work:

1. Identify within your business plan and marketing

strategy other types of businesses that would complement your offer.
2. Identify businesses that you have worked with/contacted before that would fit your business values.
3. List the types of additional services you would like to offer your clients.
4. Outline the boundaries that you are prepared to work within.
5. Arrange one-to-ones with the chosen businesses to discuss requirements and criteria.
6. Once collaboration partners are established. set clear boundaries and put an agreement in place.

Client Reviews

Look at the Operations section for more. After completing a three-month review with your clients, you can make sure that you are on track with what you're planning to deliver with them. Check that you are on track to help them achieve their goals and the brief that they have originally set with you. When you complete a three-month review it's also a great time to get feedback on how well it's going and what they're enjoying by working with you. It helps you to understand what their deeper plans are going forward in the coming months, maybe even years ahead, so that you can foresee what type of services or offerings they might need from you or from someone you know.

When we know this, we can refer them to others if need be. If you have an affiliate link or referral partner set up this can really help but a lot of business owners shy away from seeking a client review because they don't want to hear what their clients might think of them. It's a great way to understand what's going on, if anything needs to change, and to get a clear plan in place at this point.

Contingency Plan!

This is an area that you need to be mindful of. As you get traction in your business, and you start to create the business that you are looking for, you need to review your 'under the bus' contingency plan with your team. If you don't have a team, document your plan so that it's easy for someone to pick up. If something were to sadly happen to you or you had to take time out of the business unexpectedly, could someone pick up what they needed to know and do on your behalf in your business? No one's ever going to replace you, for sure, but create a plan so that someone could step in and run your business because of an emergency or an eventuality that's happened.

Ask yourself:

In your business, how is your contingency plan documented?

Where could someone find the information?

Who would you ask to step in?

What semi-passive and passive income do you have running?

D =

***Day* Job – getting out of it**

I've helped several different people get out of the day job and start running a business. This does take time and I always recommend running the setup of the new business alongside the day job as much as you possibly can. This allows you to get clear on what the business is, what the business looks like, to get in front of networking groups and ideal clients, and to share with your audience, but at the same time to have the cash flow behind you, and you do not see a dip in income. I recommend that you set a date to make the final switch from the day job to the business. You can change it if you need to: it doesn't have to be set in stone.

Find a coach or mentor, a masterminding group, or a trusted individual who can support you every step of the way, somebody who's going to challenge you, question you, and help you have a plan in place. Fundamentally, the key thing here is accountability. Find the right accountability partner to help you stay on track with such a big transition. The key part of the formula is how to keep progressing the plan to get the results.

Digital Detox

This one might scare some of you. A digital detox is when you find a space in your business during which you reflect and come away from things like social media or sending emails.

You might just have a break from responding to and engaging in social media posts. And this is okay. You don't have to be front facing and on top of social media all the time, because it can prove quite overwhelming for a lot of business owners to be constantly seeing posts and reels and stories and videos. It's not for everyone 24/7.

If this is you and you would like to be able to plan in when to take a step back and not engage as much then that's fine. I have done this myself. For example, I've spent one month not really engaging on social media and it's been a breath of fresh air. After it, I'm ready with the next stage of my ninety-day plan to get back on it and to be able to connect again with my audience. During that break I've really only posted personal, fun things that I'm doing rather than things with a business focus.

Doers and Talkers

I come up against this quite frequently in business. There is a clear divide between business owners: there are those who are the doers are those who are the talkers. The doers are the ones who have the plans, put everything into action, and they stick by their decisions. They see what works and what doesn't work and if things don't work they are willing to learn from their mistakes and make it better the next time round.

I also come across those who are just the talkers. They expect things to be easier, expect things to just fall into place and expect not to really have to put much effort into making their business a success. It's this kind of business owner that doesn't necessarily have the longevity in business, because they're not putting into place what they're talking about and not following through on their plans, and therefore they don't get the results.

* * *

E =

Business *Essentials*

Having these core essentials in place means you can always go back to the ways of working in your business that provide a clear and concise process and offering to your clients. This doesn't mean that you shouldn't grow and develop your business into different areas, levels and layers, but putting the foundations in place is important, whether you are in month/year one of your business, or whether you have been in business for years and now realise that you have been winging it for a really long time.

Link here for further details and business essential modules:https://links.nikimatyjasik.co.uk/business-essentials

Being the *Expert*

Being the expert in your field helps you stand out in a crowd, even when that crowd is noisy. Identify where you fit within the marketplace and how you support your niche of clients and businesses. Work towards being the best possible version of yourself. You can do this through working on yourself through self, personal and business development.

* * *

F =

The *Fortune* Is in the Follow Up! See Pipeline Section in Operations.

Focus - When you are clear on your vision and you are invested in your goals and are passionate about what you're doing, your focus is a given. You are fired up and ready to go. You don't need any more encouragement once you are invested and passionate. Find your focus by identifying your vision, goals and passion.

* * *

G =

Get **It Done!**

Grow **- You must continue to challenge yourself if you want to grow**

As you develop and grow in your business, you are forever facing challenges or scenarios in which you need to provide a solution that could take you out of your comfort zone. It leaves you in a place where you are unsure as to the right decision to make. To grow, step outside of your comfort zone and develop. Continue to challenge yourself in your business to grow into the type of expert and leader that you want to be.

Gratitudes

Gratitude serves you extremely well when it comes to running your business and therefore on a personal basis as well. Get into the habit, morning and evening, of capturing one to three things that you have been grateful for that day or what you will be grateful for in the day ahead. You can read more about this in the Finance part and in Personal Development too.

What you think about, you bring about; what you believe in will inevitably happen. Have those gratitudes in place and reflect on them on a weekly basis. This helps to form the positive mindset that you're looking for.

* * *

H =

Habits

Form daily habits as part of your daily routine to stay on track and to show up as your best possible self. This could be a meditation morning, stretch, or a morning blueprint, through to journalling, or sitting quietly with a herbal tea before anyone else is up in the morning. It could be going for a run, for a walk, reading a book, or getting some words out of your head and written down. They don't have to mean anything – they just need to be out of your head! Whatever kind of habit you begin, it's about applying it on a consistent basis in a positive way to set you up for the best possible day. Key words to adopt to align to those habits are being focused, taking responsibility, being consistent, being committed and stepping into your confidence.

Help - **What help do you need in your business right now?**

When things feel tough or are not flowing, or, on the flipside, when you have a plan but you don't know how to implement it or how to get the next steps in place, take a moment to step back and ask yourself these questions:

- What help do I need in my business right now?
- What is going to help me reach where I want to be?
- Is the problem something that I need to work on – mindset, perhaps?
- Do I need coaching or mentoring to help me through this time?
- Where is the flow not quite happening right now?

Review on a regular basis and have your ninety-day plan in place. This allows you to identify what help you need in the business at that point. If you're stuck on a decision or face a challenge, there is always a solution. Ask yourself what you need right now in order to make this happen.

Hold Your Nerve!

This is a biggie. Everyone has to experience it when running their business. There are going to be ups and downs, highs and lows, peaks and dips! Whichever way you want to explain it, there will be times when you are out of your comfort zone. At times you won't want to do things. Sometimes the money isn't coming through. There will be times when you don't get that client you thought you were going to get. However, if you are being consistent with your activity, showing up, being clear on your goals and what you want to achieve, unless you're doing it badly you will always find a way to get the results that you are looking for.

This has happened to me so many times in my business and it has always come good. It is a part of developing and growing in your business to be able to share your experiences and to be able to step into the next stage of your plan.

* * *

I =

Income-producing Activity

Also read the section about the qualifier question. In order to avoid distractions that come your way and to face daily challenges, ask your qualifier question of whether an activity will take you towards your goal or not. As well as that, ask whether the activity is actually an income-producing activity. Do you know that it will ultimately generate income?

What *Inspired* You to Start Your Business?

When things aren't going right or when things don't feel particularly great, I always take a few moments out to reflect and connect back with why I started my business: what inspired me to start my business in the first place? Feeling unhappy about your business normally means that you have just lost the connection with why you're doing what you're doing. Remind yourself what it was that you put in place in the first instance. Take time out to be clear about what inspired you to start your business. Was it a passion? Was it something that you saw wasn't working and you knew you could do a much better job? Was it a light bulb moment, an inspiration that you had through following somebody else? Or was it an amalgamation of ideas? Keep this close, like the vision and goals piece.

Ideal Client

Understand the type of person that you want to work with. Sometimes you don't need to look much further than yourself to determine the type of person that you want to work with. So many times, I have said to myself that I just need someone like me to help me in my business!

When you're detailing your ideal client:

- Write out twenty-five sentences about your ideal client.
- How old are they?
- Where do they live?
- What gender are they?
- Do they have children?
- Are they a certain age group and which age group?
- Are they international clients?
- Do they dress in a certain way?
- Do they drive a certain car?
- Do they eat a certain diet?

There are so many possibilities. Honing in on the types of clients you want to work with once you have established your business is essential.

In the early days of your business, you may say yes to everything to help you establish your niche and that's okay! Not everyone knows their niche from the outset.

Keep addressing your niche and ideal client on a regular basis. It could be that you want someone who aligns to your values, someone who is willing to invest time and money in themselves, someone who pays on time and respects the work you do, they value the time that you're giving to them. Keep a section within your review to check in with the types of clients you've got against that list that you have made, to ensure that they're similar.

* * *

J =

Journalling

A daily habit of journalling works well for so many business owners. It gives you a space to be able to offload and download from your mind and from your brain what is going on. Having a space to do that can be effective to help you clear your head and get clarity and to help you process with a good night's sleep. Write down what is going on and how you may be able to address things. Don't overthink this exercise. I think it's about finding a time in the day that works for you, either first thing or before bed.

Business *Journey*

Blimey, it is *such* a journey, so don't give yourself a hard time. Be prepared for that journey; it's not all going to come together from the outset, nor is it all going to come together within six or maybe even twelve months. I find that a business needs to be in place for at least three years before it can start to effectively be consistent. A lot of businesses don't make it past year three and there are several contributing factors to that.

Having a plan, working on your mindset, being consistent, having accountability, and having a method in place which you can follow monthly can really help you have the great foundations to support you. It's not going to happen overnight, and remember there are going to be a lot of ups and downs to achieving what you want to achieve.

* * *

K =

***Know*, Like, Trust**

This is key when it comes to building relationships in business. The know, like, trust factor, which I've mentioned a number of times in the book, is about being able to build a good and strong reputation within your chosen industry, so you stand out in a crowd. You show up for your clients, you are delivering to your clients, you are looking after your clients, and you are building that rapport.

* * *

L =

***Luck* is Spelt w-o-r-k**

You may hear the phrase in business, when somebody has said they are lucky or they have a certain kind of turnover in their business, or they have those types of clients, or they are travelling all over the world, or they're driving a nice car, or they have nice things. Other common phrases are imposter syndrome or FOMO (fear of missing out!) when you are focused on other people's successes. I was reminded in my network marketing days: luck is not luck – it is spelt *w-o-r-k*. The things that you see, and the things people say about successful business owners when they reach a certain level in their business come down to consistent hard work on a regular basis.

To achieve everything that I'm talking about in this book means showing up and working hard on a regular basis to achieve what you want to achieve in your business. There are lots of stories out there in which business owners say, "Come and work with me and you'll get £100,000 in six weeks." It's fair to say that types of businesses like that may not succeed. They might be a one off. They might be that type of business which achieves it once but is not consistent thereafter. To get the consistent results and the types of achievement you want in your business, it is about stepping up, working and showing up on a regular basis and that is where the luck will kick in.

Become a Good *Listener*

This is a huge skill that a lot of people forget is essential when you are in business.

Give others the space to share what they need to share. Give them the space to be able to ask the questions and work out the answers that they are looking for, and then process on their behalf what they're saying to give them the solutions or challenging questions that they need to improve.

Decide What You Want to *Let* Go of

It's all about control! I hear time and time again from clients when they are feeling overwhelmed that they're busy, but the plan just isn't coming together. Also, they may be a bit of a perfectionist. They like to be in control of every single aspect of their business.

Hints and tips on how to manage

- Work on how to process the control and the perfectionism.
- Identify where those blocks are coming up for you.
- Take time through your daily planner and some of the planning techniques that I've shown you to really understand what you need to let go of.
- What is it that you are holding on to in your business that you don't need to do, but you need somebody else to do for you?

Steep *Learning* Curve

Within your business you can feel like you are on a steep learning curve for quite some time to begin with. There's always something to learn, there's always something to develop and grow from. There are always areas where you're making mistakes and you need to learn from them and improve on them. However, this happens at every stage in your business so it doesn't matter if you're on £1000 a month starting out or you're on £10,000 a month and beyond, we are all on a steep learning curve at every stage in our business. The way that we can work with this and manage it, is if we are planned effectively. Refer to Plan, Do, Review, and Improve with the ninety-day plan to make changes and understand what actions need to take place.

Learn on the Job

It's okay to do this, to learn as you go along, running your business, learning from your mistakes and moving forward. It's impossible to know everything about running a business from the outset and to be in a space where you know every possible answer.

To find your answer to every possible challenge or query that comes up in your business journey, put yourself in a space where you can review what's going on, where you can identify what's worked well and what hasn't worked well. This means that you are always growing and developing and moving yourself and your business forward to achieve the goals you want.

* * *

M =

Money Mindset

One of the most fundamental areas in which business owners procrastinate is when they have a poor money mindset: they don't look to invest, and they can come across quite desperate at times, which can impact on their client leads and retention.

I encourage you to work on your money mindset from the outset. We hold on to beliefs and experiences from our childhoods that can limit us. Seek out either Denise Duffield Thomas or Fanny Snaith to embark on support from a money mindset / coach professional.

I urge you to make this part of your development early on in your business journey so that you are always working on this. Under the Finance section you will find certain tools and steps you can take. Regardless of the stage you are at in your business, you will encounter money mindset issues. Whether you're turning over £1000 or are a millionaire, the problems normally just shift to meet you where you are on the journey.

Meetings

Before arranging a meeting – ask yourself these questions:

- Is this necessary and does it need to be on Zoom or face to face?
- How long does this meeting need to be?

- Do I need to set the boundaries and agenda?
- Do I need to prepare anything?
- Who is taking the actions, the roles, and responsibilities? Did we agree a follow up time and date?
- Do I need to send anything else?
- Choose your setting – standing... walking... be flexible with this.

A lot of people prefer to go for a walk when having a meeting because they are out in the fresh air, they're getting some exercise, and they think a lot more clearly when they are on the move. You can also organise a meeting with part of it on Zoom and part of it around the table. During what part of a meeting will you need a break? When can you decide to take time out for thirty minutes to clear your head and then come back? This can help with your energy and focus to bring some momentum back into the meeting, particularly if it's over a long day or afternoon.

* * *

N =

Say *No* to What Does not Excite You.

This one goes without saying, really. You will get to a place as a business owner when it is okay to say no to an opportunity that doesn't excite you.

By this stage in your business, you are a lot more at your ease, more confident and have the clarity around who you want to work with. The people pleasing has stopped and the need to say yes to everything has long gone!

Don't be frightened to say no to something that really doesn't interest you and really doesn't excite you. If you feel as though it's going to drain you rather than lift you, you don't have to do it.

* * *

O =

Organisation

This is a topic I get asked about quite a lot in terms of how to best organise the admin in a business.

You might be experiencing:

- Too many emails
- Too many messages from everywhere
- Too many folders in your emails
- Confusion
- Overwhelm
- Calls at inconvenient times

Solutions to help:

- Boundaries in place regarding replying to emails
- Setting aside time (ideally at the beginning of the day and at the end of the day) to reply to messages or emails
- Putting an 'out of office' on, to set the expectation for the sender on when you will reply
- Centralising your messages into a few places, but confirming with your clients how you will communicate
- Moving folders from email into Trello or Asana to keep information logged by client or project

Working *On* Your Business Rather Than in It

Many business owners only find time to work *in* their business, delivering every aspect of their service to their clients and meeting the demands of others, while forgetting that they need to spend time working *on* it too.

Plan time to focus on business development. Made sure that you have enough support in your business, whether that is from team members, a coach, a mentor, or masterminding group, to focus on your plans and be really engaged with what's happening in the months ahead. Use your ninety-day plan and your review to make sure you are not repeating mistakes. Address the challenges in your business, improve on them and keep moving forwards.

Just think: if your clients left and you had spent all your time working for them and no time filling your pipeline, you would be starting from scratch to build your clients again. 80% client, 20% business development – always!

* * *

P =

Ninety-day *Planning*

Set aside a clear half day or day every ninety days to review your previous ninety days and to plan the ninety days ahead.

Have clear goals on where you want to be financially, in business, personally, and in your learning. You can then continue to achieve these levels in your business to achieve your overall goal at the end of the year.

Examples of your goals:

- launch a particular service
- begin running an agency
- hit a certain income bracket
- grow your audience to a certain size

All your goals are broken down over the year into blocks of activity to help you move towards that final goal at the end of the year.

Finalise your ninety-day goals first, then break them down

into the activities you need to do to make the goal happen. You can use your planning structure to take your plans into your monthly, weekly and daily planning.

A ninety-day plan gives you a solid view on month one, an idea and an outline for month two, and allows you to have an eye on month three. You can always add to it and update it. You can also complete a rolling month to keep your plans moving forwards.

Personal Touch, Personal Outreach

One of my favourite ways to connect with people or businesses is through personal outreach.

Provide a personal touch when communicating. Reach out with a phone call or booking a call, so that you don't do everything over DMs or online.

Sometimes all that person needs is to have that warm connection in a conversation that's going to answer all their questions – as they have been sitting on the fence about working with you. It gives them the certainty and clarity they need to want to work with you. Personal outreach is key in terms of wanting to support that client or that individual in order to get the best outcome.

Profiling

You can use profiling in line with your ideal client work. It gives you an extra layer to look more in depth at certain enquiries or opportunities. Sometimes you must profile further to discover whether a person fits your ideal client status and whether you do or don't want to work with them. It helps you make your decision.

Activity in Your *Pipeline*

Your pipeline should always be flowing. It's a numbers game. Get as many people as possible into the funnel at whichever level is appropriate. Clients will make their decision to work with you at different stages of their journey, based on cost, timings, and on headspace. Make sure you have a strong flow of ten to twenty people active in your pipeline (or 'hotties' as I like to call them) at any one time.

***Personal*- and Self-Development**

Your Relationship with Yourself

This is an area to recognise and work on regularly, not only within your business but on a personal level. As you grow and develop in your business and in your life, you can start to see a change, maybe in your patterns or your habits. You may have a different outlook or different mindset. It is massively beneficial to be aware of these at different stages and to work on them with the right support in place.

You can feel stuck, isolated, overwhelmed, and out of your comfort zone. By using someone in your business such as a life coach, a spiritual coach, an EFT or NLP coach or a hypnotherapist you can deal with the blocks and understand what is going on. It allows you to put the next self-development or personal development plans or structures in place to help you manage and to focus correctly on what you want to deliver in your business and personally.

Add personal and self-development into your ninety-day plan. Focus on how to look after yourself and how to continually be working on yourself, to help align yourself to deliver positively in your business and in life too. This way, you are building into your plan the development you need to show up at every stage of your business.

Identify any training that you need to plan in, potentially with a budget, so that it can be forecasted within your business. An area you might forget as a business owner is how you can deal with the blocks and get even better at running your business.

- Approach with passion and determination.
- Make that promise to yourself.
- Believe in yourself.
- Do not fall short of your potential.
- Use your power to change someone's life.
- Let go of disappointment.
- Learn from mistakes and adjust your course.
- Reduce your recovery time.
- Regardless of how bad things are right now, there is light at the end of the tunnel. Have a plan, grow, transform, and find your flow.

Q =

Questions – See FAQs Pages 99 - 102

* * *

R =

Handling *Rejections*

We are not all great at handling rejection and having people say no.

One thing that helps (a great mentor, Jan Ruhe, shared this) is to write down the 4 SWs:

- **Some will**
- **Some won't**
- **So what?**
- **Someone is waiting!**

A great way to handle rejection, when someone says no is to remember that no just means 'no for now' not 'no forever'. Circumstances change, situations change and inevitably they will need a service – either yours or a similar one at some stage. Continuing to build that relationship is really important. If somebody says no to you, I recommend saying, "I understand. Let's reconnect in three months' time." They may be in a different place by then.

Routine

Read **a book for ten mins every day (routine)**

As part of your daily routine, you could do something like reading a book for ten minutes. This could be a personal development book, a self-development book, or it could be a business book.

Reading these kinds of non-fiction books can help you to feel creative and to gain inspiration so that you can work through your ideas, thoughts, or exciting opportunities.

I suggest watching box sets and movies – watching different formats can spur creativity and inspiration.

How I start my day and why (routine)

Set yourself a morning routine that you can get into. Do the same things in order to start the day in the best possible way for you. A morning routine really can set you up for the day and put you in the right mindset. It can send you in the positive direction that you want to go, in order to achieve your activities and tasks and interactions for the day.

You could start your day with:

- Meditation
- A mini blueprint
- Yoga or the gym
- A cup of herbal tea and a couple of pages of your favourite book

- Journalling

When you put together a morning routine before you enter your working day, it's important to identify what works for you.

A lot of people don't watch the news in the morning because they don't want to start with a negative impact on the day.

Try a morning routine for three months and review what works for you.

What challenges you every day? (routine)

Summarise your challenges at the end of every day. This will help you to see a pattern of what is happening in your business or what's happening for yourself. This helps you to see solutions to make these challenges so much easier. The flipside of this question could be what challenges you *want* every day. How do you want to step out your comfort zone? How do you want to show up? Is there a new method or a new way or a new emphasis that you want to set in place for yourself, your business, and your clients? It's about challenging yourself.

***Referral* Partners**

Seek out the right referral partners who know and have worked with you or people you are working with in order to help refer on their behalf.

Arranging a commission or a financial agreement on any secured business can work well for a lot of different business types. It helps you to get people out there bringing in business for you on your behalf.

Carefully consider the types of referral partners you would like to have in place and why. Approach them and see where the conversation can take you in terms of setting up partnerships.

Retainers

Regular income from monthly retainers is a way to build your business. A retainer is an agreement by which you consistently work with that client over a certain period. Think about the type of client that you would want to work with and what your retainer brief would be.

When you consider offering retainers it is normally at the higher end of your model. Clients are limited on time or want to invest more and want to have a more VIP or higher-level experience.

* * *

S =

Screen **Your Calls**

For more on this, read about the qualifier question and about setting boundaries. I speak from experience in running my business that screening my phone calls can be a top time saver.

I recommend that you schedule in any phone calls from new enquiries, clients, or your team.

If a phone number or a call comes up that I'm not expecting, I let that call go to voicemail. I pick it up at a time that suits me and then I communicate with that person so that they get an update in response to the message and they can book a phone call if need be. It is easy to get distracted when this happens, but setting the boundaries allows you to remain focused on your daily goal.

Shiny Objects

I hear time and time again that business owners don't focus on a plan. They don't focus on where they want to be and what they want to achieve, because they're too busy getting shiny object syndrome. They are constantly reviewing out in the marketplace what is available to buy, what has been launched, and they are doing another course. They don't have time to do it, or maybe even the money to invest, but people want what others have.

***Slight* Edge**

I adopted this really early on in my business. It's actually from my network marketing days, based on a book called *The Slight Edge* by Jeff Olson.

It really helps break down how approaching everything on a regular basis, daily, means that you approach tasks consistently rather than rushing things or being in a place where it's not flowing.

Semi-passive or Passive Income

The online world has landed in many businesses now, bringing semi-passive or passive incomes into our businesses. This can be a great business addition to support the ongoing development of your business.

Semi-passive or passive incomes sources include:

- **Courses – live and evergreen**
- **Memberships**
- **Affiliates**
- **Payment plans**
- **Books and workbooks**
- **Masterminds**
- **Influencer agreements**
- **Subscription boxes**

Within your ninety-day planning structure, review where and when you can bring in semi-passive or passive income ideas.

Support Network

When it comes to running your business, you can't be everywhere, doing everything and being everything to everyone. Understand in your business and in your life what support you need and where you can find it.

Break these support needs down into your business requirements and personal requirements to help stay on track.

Where could you need support?

- Family
- Team
- Clients
- Friends
- Cleaner
- Online food delivery

In preparation for your week ahead, ask yourself what support you need around you to be able to show up as your best self in your business and personally.

Seasons

This isn't for everyone. However, I have seen time and time again that a lot of business owners work better at certain times of the year. Personally, I am more productive in my business from March to November. Make this a consideration in your business.

You can expect to experience what sits with your own feelings and personality.

As business owners we are guided to be ready for January, and then we are told that September is the new January. Times have changed and approaches have changed regarding how we plan and review our businesses to reflect ourselves and our personalities.

Rather than going for it in January and setting goals and putting New Year's resolutions in place during the winter period, it might suit you better to sit in a time of hibernation. It might be a better time to reflect and take stock of what's been happening in your business and in your life.

You might then see the shoots of the spring; this is when a lot of business owners start to pop their heads up from underneath the duvet. Transitioning into March and April around springtime provides many of us with a real boost.

This energy, momentum, focus and flow can last all the way through to late summer or autumn. From Halloween onwards, business owners start to review the year and understand what they need to put in place for the coming year. Then over the winter months they start to process what that can look like.

Some business owners move their business with the seasons into other countries, making the spring and summer time a consistent part of their plans. Whichever way you approach this in your business, we all need a period to reflect, recharge and refocus. Find the time that suits you.

- Nourish yourself in the winter.
- Make plans in the spring.
- Get outside in the summer.
- Seek self-care in the autumn.

Structure

Thinking and Processing

Create space in the day, between working for your clients and working on your business, for you to have thinking and processing time. We tend to get caught up in running our business and providing the right ideas, solutions, and outcomes for our clients. If we keep doing this and never step away, we can just be moving from one task to the next to the next.

Build time in for thinking and processing, and highlight this to your clients. They may only see the time that they are paying you for. For example, if they book a two-hour session, they may not see the additional time that you spend thinking, processing, and preparing ahead of it.

Take back the first half hour of the day (structure)

Plan to have the first hour or half hour of the day to kick off your daily routine. When you start the day with your own actions means you are completing the parts you need for your business to flourish. This sets the tone for the day. It helps you to liaise with team members, schedule social media, answer emails or enquiries and complete the most important tasks.

. . .

Surrounding Yourself

It is said we become the five people we hang out with. Therefore, choose these five people wisely. Make sure those five people are there to lift you, support you and believe in you.

Exercise:

- Identify the people you currently surround yourself with. Are they suitable?
- Make a list of those you would like to surround yourself with?
- Write a profile: for example, are they smart, successful, great dressers, positive, likeminded, focused, driven?
- Surround yourself with those who see greatness within you.
- Check your last five messages or calls. Who were they to or from?

Skills and Attitudes

- What do I need in terms of skills to run my business?
- What do I need as the right attitudes in my business?

Answering these questions can help you be clear on:

1. How you show up as your best self.

2. How you show up as an expert in your field.
3. How you show up not only to serve your clients but also when you're talking with likeminded business owners.
4. How you approach meetings and networking.

Exercise:

Take a piece of paper and brainstorm:

- What you believe are the skills you need to have
- What you believe are the right attitudes

Example:

A skill could be listening, speaking, communication, teamwork, problem solving, leadership.

An attitude could be positivity, focus, motivation, enthusiasm, kindness, hope.

Spend time breaking this down to be clear on which skills and attitudes you have in place for your business and to identify where you might need support or help to learn new skills.

There Is Always a *Solution*

Whatever you are in your business journey, whatever your challenges, whatever questions are being thrown up and presented to you, there is always a solution.

The best way to deal with a challenge or situation in your business is:

- Initially step away from it
- Digest and process what the situation is and what is going on
- Go for a walk
- Sleep on it

By not responding in haste (emergencies are the exception) the right solution can always be found. The solution you decide on may not feel comfortable to begin with, but trust your gut instinct, knowledge, and experience to deliver the best outcome.

* * *

T =

Time Management

When is the best *time* of the day for you to work?

Ask yourself when during the day you are most productive. Align this with your default and vision diary.

Depending on your commitments, seek to find that sweet spot of productivity. That might be starting at seven or eight in the morning, and then seeing the first client at ten, or it might be fitting it around children at school or around a day job.

Try the method for a month and see what does and doesn't work for you.

Schedule your down*time*

Bring downtime within your default and vision diary schedule. Align this to your ninety-day plan and have a section where self-care, family time and holidays are planned in.

The ninety-day plan helps you to be structured in the business to achieve time off and this means you can step away from the business, switch off, regenerate and be more creative when you return to your business.

Run a *time* audit

When you feel overwhelmed, frustrated, or you're busy but you're not making the progress in your business that you want, I suggest you set up a time tracking tool such as Toggl or the daily planner. Over a two-week period, track where you spend most of your business time.

Ask yourself:

- Am I spending too much time on tasks?

- Am I doing tasks that I shouldn't be doing?
- Am I procrastinating on tasks?
- Am I spending too much time with clients?
- Am I giving too much time to my networking one-to-ones?

You can start to review what is and what isn't working in your business, and where you can eliminate and reduce the overwhelm and frustration.

Schedule *time* in chunks

Colour coding and segmenting your business and personal times into chunks can provide a productive schedule.

Examples:

8-10am – business development and marketing time.

Client time starts at 10am.

Keep certain tasks and activities to set times.

Time blocking can help create flow, momentum and focus on what you need to do.

Choose your hours, and be flexible (time)

When running your own business, one area that can be attractive is your ability to choose your own hours. You can be flexible on how you work, where you work, and what your circumstances are. Your business hours can fit around school hours, locations, family commitments, holidays or another business, job, or project.

Perhaps you're new to business, or you feel that you have become stuck with a certain scenario in your business. You may know you want to work less or you have a period of time when you want to work more so you can gain the flexibility and time off in the future. Plan and then review this within your ninety-day structure, seeing what does and doesn't work for you. At first, you are everything to everyone in your business. As your business grows and develops you can start to outsource. This is another opportunity to choose the hours you work and gain flexibility.

Business *Toolkits*

Identify which toolkits in particular you need within your business to help you maintain your effectiveness on a regular basis. This could be around business planning or around social media planning. It could be top tips on addressing visibility, marketing, accounting, speaking or knowing your numbers. There are lots of different toolkits out there and lots of different books. Identify, on a regular monthly basis, what you need to support you and then determine the types of toolkits you need in place to help.

* * *

U =

Understanding Personality Types

Understanding personality types takes a lot of practice but when you are building a business, it can save you time, energy, and money because you understand how to deal with different types of people.

Understanding personalities can benefit you, your client, your one-to-ones, your collaborations, and your supplier relationships, giving you the opportunity to provide the best possible service and business.

There are different methods you could use:

Personality Colour Types: Red – Directional; Yellow – Inspirational; Blue – Operational; Green – Collaborative

Myers & Briggs

Chinese Horoscopes

DISC Module

* * *

V =

Vision Diary

It is important to build up to a vision diary covering different stages in your business. As you achieve certain goals and plans in your business, it's important to review the structure of your day, week, and month in your business. Again, use the simple default diary format or a monthly calendar format download version here: https://links.nikimatyjasik.co.uk/accountability-toolkit you can start to set how your time can look. For example, eventually you might want to work half days, school hours, take a day off a week, or every other Friday off. Putting this down on paper allows you to visualise what it could be like, and your activities can support you to achieve this.

Vulnerability

This can be a tough one to admit to and talk about as a business owner. Being open and showing vulnerability can be challenging for most.

I've certainly experienced the difficulties around this. However, having elements of openness and vulnerability about yourself means your clients and your audience are likely to find you relatable. You might share a situation, problem, or challenge with your audience to connect with them and discuss it with them. They may be going through something very similar and by hearing you they feel they are not alone.

Hearing that somebody else is going through the same will really help you to build relationships through the know, like, trust factor.

I would like to be clear; this isn't about exposing every single part of you and your life in your business.

It's about sharing:

- Whether you're having a bad day
- Whether you've not seen the success that you thought you would
- Whether a client has not converted
- Whether you've lost your mojo that week

Remember: People buy people. And without being icky, we can connect with our audience and ideal client through genuinely sharing the highs and lows.

Imagine looking back over your life (vision)

Create a space in your journal, in your day, or in your favourite place where you can visualise looking back over your life.

Ask Yourself:

- What would you have wanted to achieve?
- What do you want to be known for?
- What legacy do you want to leave?
- What do you want people to be saying about you?
- How would people remember you at your funeral?

I don't mean to sound sad here. This exercise can help you focus on:

- What your passions are
- What you are missing in your life
- What you want to achieve in business or personally

* * *

W =

Prioritise your *Wellbeing*

I can't emphasise this enough. I know you need to work hard to develop a business, but you also need to look after your wellbeing.

I come from a corporate background where if you weren't working – why weren't you working? If you weren't getting results – why weren't you getting results? It was very much a cut-throat kind of job. I have learnt to prioritise my wellbeing as a business owner. You are your business and if you are not at your best then you will not be able to deliver to yourself, your family/support network, or to your clients.

It is a fundamental part of the ninety-day plan to have a self-care and wellbeing plan in place alongside your business, personal and self-development plan.

Ideas:

- Gym/exercise
- Sleep
- Reduce alcohol, sugar, watch your nutrition and supplements
- Yoga retreats
- Meditation retreats
- Have time and space to read
- Get out in nature
- Go to your favourite beach
- Shopping (a firm favourite of mine!)

WDYKL (*Who* Do You Know List)

Another part of your pipeline work is to build a *Who do you know?* list. When you are launching a new service or offer, or you need to connect with clients in a certain way or connect with prospects in a certain way, it can help you get communications out to several people whom you understand could be interested in your services.

***Work* from Anywhere**

The pandemic has proven how successful working from home can be. We have now moved forward to being able to work from anywhere in the world with more ease than ever before.

- Take the opportunity to plan being flexible in your locations, whether that means working from home or when you are abroad.
- Be flexible in your approach with your clients and your style.
- Fit your business around your hobbies.
- Research spaces.
- This approach could help you stand out amongst others in the marketplace by showing that you provide flexibility to your clients and network.
- This way of working can keep the passion, energy, inspiration, innovation, and creativity at the heart of what you do.
- You get the chance to connect with your local communities – your clients can be right under your nose!

* * *

X =

***X-Rayed* Insight – Refer to Plan, Do, Review and Improve; Sales and Marketing, People, Operations and Finance.**

* * *

Y =

Invest in *Yourself*

Build investment in yourself into your plan and budgets from the start of your business.

Working *on* your business not just *in* it all the time is a fundamental solution that business owners often overlook.

Investing in training, personal development, business development and growth can be perceived as expensive, and often the business owner wants to be making a certain level of income first. Sometimes a business owner feels they can do everything on their own. Everyone soon comes to realise that this is not the case.

When I started my business back in 2015, I tried to do everything myself for the first year. I quickly saw that I just could not do it all on my own. I decided to start working with a business coach. I had no idea how I was going to pay for it, but I knew I would find a way. Warning: This method does not suit everyone!

This meant that every single month I had to achieve enough client conversions to ensure that I could cover the fee for my business coach. After a few months, once my confidence, clarity and business started to grow, I complemented the coaching by joining a mastermind group. The balance of the two helped me stay focused, accountable, and achieving my goals. When I started out in my business, I had to take three part time jobs alongside my business to have cash flow. I was able to give these roles up within six months of working with the business coach.

Benefits of the business coach and masterminding group combo:

- Consistent turnover
- Focus
- Motivation
- Accountability
- Confidence
- Clarity
- Structure
- Business growth
- Strong reputation

Fast forward to date in my business, now that it's grown to six figure turnovers. I wanted to learn more skills and different approaches to be able to work with my ideal clients both on and offline. I have invested even greater amounts into my business through high level masterminding, and one to one coaching and mentoring sessions.

Whichever stage you're at in your business, start *somewhere* by investing in what you need to take you out of your comfort zone, free up the areas that you may be controlling in your business, and you need to let go of. You will then step into the best version of yourself and deliver the type of business that you want to run with the type of flexibility and freedom you want.

* * *

Z =

Zealous **Thoughts**

Reignite the spark!

When running your business, you can lose direction and your mojo.

One of the most frequent questions I get asked by business owners is:

How do I get out of my own way and stop procrastinating in my business?

Solutions:

- Reconnecting yourself with your passion
- Reconnecting yourself with who your ideal client is
- Working on your mindset – what is the block?
- Finding a sounding board to vocalise your challenges.

Consider every detail

Ask Questions; Ask Questions; Ask Questions!

Embed the habit of asking questions in your business from the outset.

You are busy, in a rush, and because of this when making decisions in your business you might go with the first solution you find and don't give yourself the time to explore other opportunities.

This approach will feel time consuming at first, but when you get into the flow of it, you end up saving yourself time, money and energy *and* you get the best possible solutions and decisions made for your business.

Solutions:

- Give yourself time to consider every detail when investing in your business.
- Do your research and due diligence for each quote, investment, or enquiry you make for support in your business.
- Check out their testimonials and reviews.
- Compare quotes like for like as much as you can.
- Ask all the questions that feel right to fulfil your brief, particularly if you are unsure of the information provided or you need further explanation.
- Ask for referrals and references from your support network.
- If all else fails, go with your gut instinct.

Find your niche.

There are two ways to approach this question when you first start out in business or are reviewing it for the first time on your business journey.

When you start out in business you might want to say yes to everything that comes your way. This helps you to determine the types of clients you do and don't want to work with in the short, medium, and long term.

Or you could be specific about your niche from the start. You might want to navigate your way and take your time to get the right ideal clients on board.

Before you start making money in your business, whichever route you decide to go down as a business owner, you will find your niche eventually, because we all do.

- Continue to review your niche.
- Continue to review your ideal client.
- Ask yourself which types of clients excite or interest you.
- Ask yourself who you want to connect with and who is aligned with your boundaries.
- Ask yourself which types of clients are aligned to your values.

Over time, this task gets easier and easier. As business owners, we are always aligning, growing, and developing.

Maintain your network.

Networking is a long game!

Here are my hints and tips to maintaining your network to consistently achieve results:

- Even when you are busy, keep consistent with your networking.
- Show up for everyone in the group.
- Stay connected with everyone in the group.
- Celebrate success with each other.
- Continue to share referrals.
- Stay consistent in building relationships with existing members, new members and visitors.

Find your Tribe.

You have your networking…

You have your clients…

You have people who refer to you…

You have your raving fans…

But finding your tribe at every stage in your business journey is essential.

As your business grows and develops, you end up hanging out with different business owners at different stages. This is okay. Everyone develops and grows into different levels.

Your personal development and self-development change during these stages, and you want to be able to hang out with the types that will lift you.

Keep it Simple.

Do not complicate and confuse the information you put out to your audience regarding your offers, services, and messaging.

You don't want people to be turned off by confusing messaging when they look into buying from you.

The best way to ensure you align with simplicity in your business is to ask yourself the following question:

If I said this to a seven-year-old, would they understand it?

Get Clarity

It takes time to get clarity in your business and in yourself. Once it clicks into place, the snowball effect of growth, momentum, flow and confidence begins, and you start to feel reassured that you are on the right track.

Everyone can have wobbles in their business. However, when you have the clarity on your messaging, offers and services, the flow is unstoppable.

Solutions:

- Use the Plan, Do, Review, and Improve Process.
- Discover which of these four areas are not aligned –

Sales and Marketing, People, Operations, and Finance.
- For insight and feedback, reach out to trusted individuals in your support network.
- Use a sounding board such as a coach, mentor, or accountability masterminding group. They can hold the space for you to continue honing your clarity and confidence.
- Keep aligned with your ideal client and messaging.
- Stay away from distractions to keep you on the path towards to your goals.

part e: there is no magic secret

When it comes to running a business there is no magic secret. However, from running and building my business through word of mouth, recommendation and referral over the past seven years and growing it from being in debt to a six-figure turnover, I know that the methods of this book work. Running your own business is bloody hard work but if you can find what works for you, trust in your approach and your ability, and you show up, you will get the consistent results you are looking for.

Use this book as your go-to. Find the solution to your challenge today.

My Top Tips:

- Ask yourself what you have learnt, **RELEARNT** or been reminded of.

- Be **CONSISTENT** in your activity.
- Be clear on your **VISION AND GOALS.**
- Be clear on your **WHY.**
- Set **BOUNDARIES** in your business and personal life to maintain good levels of balance.
- **SHOW UP EVERY DAY!** Even when it's tough.
- Keep on **LEARNING** – whether that is through reading, courses, podcasts, or attending seminars. **KEEP EXPANDING YOUR KNOWLEDGE** to be the best possible version of you. Ultimately this will support you, your clients, and the environment around you.
- Use methods to **STAY ON TRACK** hourly, daily, weekly, monthly, and quarterly.
- Have a **SOUNDING BOARD** whether that is a coach, mentor, networking group or a business bestie. You might consider one of these or a combination. Having this support in your business can mean you have a safe space to work through your challenges, from the easiest of questions to the toughest of decisions.
- **GO THAT EXTRA MILE** – I stand by this 100%. How you show up and serve your clients and your fellow business owners can be a game changer or a deal breaker. I believe that by going that extra mile every time (within your set boundaries) you will stand out in a crowd and be the go-to option over many others – because you helped, supported, and showed up.

part e: there is no magic secret

- You have read at length about your pipeline, 'hotties' and how to manage the flow of contacts and enquiries. But the magic truly happens in getting super clear and consistent on how **THE FORTUNE IS IN THE FOLLOW UP** Get good at this. Build those relationships, make great notes, and plan to follow up. Don't be annoying, don't be icky or persistent, just check in when it feels right; a no is not a no forever, it's just for now. Timing is everything when you are converting a client. Your client has to be ready to make the investment in terms of time and money so you can support them on the journey they want to take.
- Be **CONGRUENT, AUTHENTIC, HONEST, GENIUNE** – adopting this approach will pay you back time and time again. Showing up, being yourself, and sticking by what your values are and what you believe in speaks volumes. When you are authentic, you don't have to worry about being caught out. Build the know, like, trust factor and you will create a strong, solid foundation for your business to flourish and grow from. A good reputation and genuine warmth are priceless.
- When you have used this book as much you can and you have got the consistent results in your business, you are **READY** for the next stage.
- Good luck, have **FUN**, work smart and keep it simple!

acknowledgements

Where do I even start with this?

Writing a book (over what feels like forever) has been a massive out of comfort zone experience for me. It has needed focus, time, dedication, and learning a whole new skill… and a lot of chocolate to help me through!

Never have I procrastinated so much on a task in my business. But it is finally here! So, I am going to start with thanking myself. It's been a tough start to 2022, navigating my way to the next stage in my business. Sometimes I never thought I would get this far.

I am much more of a talker when it comes to explaining solutions to business owners and writing has never been my thing. And this fascinating process has led me to this point to help and support even more business owners, whether you are new to business or have been on your journey for a while.

First, I would like to thank my amazing sisters, Sarah, and Cazzie. You are both beyond amazing. Thank you so much for picking me up, dusting me off and supporting me. I love you both so much!

To my fantastic operations manager, Sarah Newland. You have helped me so much on this journey over the past eighteen months. You have helped me take my business to the next stage and supported me through the tough parts. Thank you for sticking with me and for your support with this book.

To my coaches, mentors, and buddies from masterminding and networking who I have known during my seven-year journey, thank you for believing in me and holding the space when I needed it the most to grow my business and myself.

To my loving family, for supporting me and giving me the space to get on with my business.

To my truly amazing, amazing clients, raving fans, and support network. I wouldn't be where I am now without your belief and trust in my methods, approach, and style.

And finally, to my gorgeous husband Lance and daughter Charlotte, who have always believed in me, held my hand, supported me, and always said, "Off you go, do your thing, we've got you." I love you both so very, very much!

work with niki

You can access Niki's world in several ways. Find the support you need at the level you need it.

You can get involved with The Business Chat on Facebook.

https://links.nikimatyjasik.co.uk/the-business-chat

You can find great tools to help you stay accountable and on track with the Accountability Toolkit.

https://links.nikimatyjasik.co.uk/accountability-toolkit

You can take it a stage further to create even more consistent results in your business with a Plan, Do, Review, and Improve workbook and online course Business Essentials.

https://links.nikimatyjasik.co.uk/workbook

https://links.nikimatyjasik.co.uk/business-essentials

work with niki

Details of all courses, speaking opportunities, events, accountability pods, mastermind groups, masterclasses, and Strategy days, and how to work one-to-one with Niki book in here:

https://links.nikimatyjasik.co.uk/home

about the author

Niki Matyjasik is a seasoned masterminder, queen of accountability, and master of getting results by making and putting into action a plan.

She works with her clients through one-to-one coaching, high level masterminding, and Group Strategy days, as well as running networking and accountability groups.

She helps her clients to create a plan, providing them with a proven framework for them to create month on month success and giving them the accountability, they need to maintain and smash their goals.

Niki is a mum to one teenager and her business journey has taken her from being significantly in debt to a six-figure turnover. She shares with her clients the step by step method of what is truly possible and walks her talk with authenticity and great leadership.

Niki comes from a retail corporate background as a buyer, project manager and category manager. She has seen business at every stage and every level.

You're in safe hands.

FACEBOOK:

https://links.nikimatyjasik.co.uk/the-business-chat

instagram.com/nikijmatyjasik

linkedin.com/in/niki-matyjasik-744ba5b3

Lightning Source UK Ltd.
Milton Keynes UK
UKHW040148041122
411612UK00007B/158/J

9 781915 771049